A
WINDOW
ON
WASHINGTON

EDWARD HUGHES PRUDEN

VANTAGE PRESS
New York   Washington   Atlanta   Hollywood

The author gratefully acknowledges permission to quote from:

> *Memoirs*, by W. A. Visser 't Hooft. Published jointly by SCM Press Ltd., London, and The Westminster Press, Philadelphia, 1973. Copyright © 1973.
>
> *The New York Times*, Copyright © 1976, by The New York Times Company.

922.6
P 971 w

To Mae
who played a major
role in the events
recorded here

CONTENTS

Preface

PREFACE

For thirty-two years as pastor of the First Baptist Church in Washington, I did much of my work in a study with large windows opening out on Sixteenth Street. This historic thoroughfare has been called "The Avenue of the Presidents," possibly because the White House is at the southern end of the street. As one emerges from the front door of the White House, he faces Sixteenth Street, which extends all the way to the Maryland state line. On this street are numerous significant institutions—the Hay-Adams House; St. John's Episcopal Church, where many presidents have worshipped; the Statler-Hilton Hotel; the Russian embassy; the National Geographic buildings; the headquarters of the National Education Association; the University Club; the Carnegie Foundation building; the National Wildlife Foundation; the Australian embassy; and numerous others. Our church is located in the midst of these institutions, and is just eight blocks from the White House. Frequently, as I sat at my desk, I would hear the sirens approaching, and looking out on Sixteenth Street, would see the president's car passing, surrounded by a police squadron on motorcycles; or the car of a foreign diplomat or visiting dignitary on his way to an embassy reception. So, symbolically, from this vantage point I watched the Washington scene go by, and occasionally had a small part in it.

While what I have written is in a sense a personal story, actually it involves a host of wonderful people—church officials, associates on the church staff, friends and members of the congregation, and public officials I met from time to time. One volume would be insufficient to relate all that I owe to them. And certainly any story in which I am involved is the story of my family. Their full participation in the life of our church, the encouragement they constantly provide, and the joy and satisfaction they give to me are very much a part of all that is recorded here. A special word of thanks is due to my wife, who offered many helpful suggestions in the preparation of the manuscript, and who did the proofreading for me.

I am grateful, too, to Elton Trueblood, my friend for many years, for reading the first draft of the manuscript and offering encouragement for the undertaking.

Appreciation is expressed also to Ethel Huskey, a member of my former church in Washington, and to Ellen Brooks, Judy White, Madge Dillard, and Karen Youngblood, secretaries at Meredith College, for their valuable assistance in typing portions of the manuscript.

Edward Hughes Pruden

January 21, 1975
Raleigh, North Carolina

I

EVANGELIZING A PARADE

Franklin D. Roosevelt was elected to his second term as president of the United States in November, 1936. Two weeks earlier, I had been called to be pastor of the First Baptist Church in Washington. Little did we know at that time how much the decisions of this man in the White House would affect the life of each one of us in the years ahead. I had a general idea of the peculiar problems and challenges which a pastorate in the nation's capital would present, but I could not possibly foresee to what extent the crises to come would complicate and accentuate every phase of my ministry.

I shall never forget the sensation I had as the skyline of Washington came into view when I approached the city to assume my new responsibilities. Soon after passing through Alexandria, Virginia, I saw in the distance the top of the Washington Monument; a few minutes later, the dome of the Capitol; and within a few minutes more, the Lincoln Memorial and the unfinished Washington Cathedral. Suddenly, I thought of the numerous embassies and the thousands of foreign nationals employed by them; the members of Congress and their staffs; the far-reaching decisions made in such a place; and the only words I could think of were, "Who is equal to these things?" As I began to wonder to what extent I was prepared to exercise an intelligent and helpful ministry in a situation of these proportions, I found some consolation in the thought that probably no preparation is adequate for such a task apart from actual participation in the life of such a community. I knew that there would be ample opportunity for this in the months ahead, and that since all men have a common Creator, our basic needs and objectives are essentially the same, and therefore differences in language, nationality, and race are purely incidental.

My journey from the small town in southern Virginia in which I was born[1] to the nation's capital had been a circuitous one, and while I had never thought of serving a church in such a cosmopolitan place, in retrospect I can pinpoint now certain circumstances and personalities which awakened in me an interest in the political process, in the people of other countries, and in the problems which affect the whole world. For instance, while still in elementary school, my interest in presidential elections was aroused when my father travelled to Washington to be present at the inauguration of Woodrow Wilson in 1913. The fact that he had been such an ardent supporter of Mr. Wilson's candidacy, and would take the time and go to the expense which such a trip required, made me feel that both Mr. Wilson and what he stood for were important.

During the time I was in high school, President Wilson was waging his gigantic struggle to persuade the people of the United States to become a part of the League of Nations which he had helped to create. When I entered college, the professor who stimulated and influenced me most[2] was an enthusiastic admirer of Mr. Wilson and a severe critic of those in the United States Senate who seemed determined to thwart the president's efforts to have our country accept membership in the League. I shall never forget the tribute paid by this professor to Mr. Wilson at a memorial service for the late president a few days after his death. The service was held in historic St. Paul's Episcopal Church in Richmond—the church Jefferson Davis and Robert E. Lee had attended

1. Chase City, in Mecklenburg County.
2. Dr. Samuel Chiles Mitchell, professor of history.

during the days of the Confederacy. As the speaker dealt with the opposition which certain United States senators had marshaled against the League proposal, especially Senator Henry Cabot Lodge of Massachusetts, his flushed face betrayed the deep emotions he felt, and then he concluded by saying: "My four sons served their country in the armed forces during the recent World War, and each of them served in a different branch of the service; but if another war should erupt due to the failure of the United States to join the League of Nations, I would want my four sons to deal with Henry Cabot Lodge!"

When I entered seminary, my professor of Greek, Dr. A. T. Robertson, had been one of the first to suggest the formation of a Baptist World Alliance. The president of the seminary, Dr. E. Y. Mullins, was president of the Alliance at the time I enrolled, and had made trips to Europe to visit Baptist bodies there. The director of the seminary choir to which I belonged, Bela Udvarnoki, was a student from Hungary, and there were other students from Sweden, Rumania, Brazil, and Australia. In addition, we had missionaries on furlough who were in residence for a few months, and occasional speakers from abroad.

All of these experiences played a part in my desire to do graduate theological work abroad, and, at the University of Edinburgh, under the influence of men like Dr. Hugh Ross Mackintosh, I continued to accumulate these wider interests and concerns which later proved to be of great help to me as I sought to minister to a church set down in the midst of what many consider to be the "crossroads of the world."

However, the greatest experience of all in this process of preparation for Washington came after five years in my first pastorate. Two years after our marriage, my wife and I were unexpectedly given an opportunity to go to China for a year and teach in the University of Shanghai. The year was 1935 and the invitation came at one of the few times in the period of China's agonizing upheaval when such a trip would have been possible. The University was supported jointly by the Northern and the Southern Baptist Conventions, and the faculty included Chinese nationals and appointees of both Conventions. The occasion which made our one-year appointment possible was the observance in China of the one hundredth anniversary of the arrival of the first missionary from Virginia, and the Virginia Baptist women were anxious to have a couple represent them during the year of this celebration. Since Chinese university students in those days possessed a rather remarkable knowledge and use of the English language, we were able to teach our classes in English. My wife, who is a graduate of the Cincinnati Conservatory of Music in piano, taught some English courses and music, and I taught English courses entirely.

The windows of our classrooms overlooked the Whangpoo River, and as we were teaching, we frequently saw the ships from many nations passing our campus on their way to Shanghai harbor, reminding us anew of the international character of that great city. Our contacts with missionaries from other countries; with business and diplomatic representatives from abroad; and with alumni of the University who were occupying places of leadership in the nation at that time—all were stimulating and broadening experiences. Visits to Ningpo, Hangchow, Canton, Soochow, Nanking, Peking, and the Great Wall enlarged our knowledge of Chinese life and history, and friendships which developed between us and the Chinese people left an indelible impression of kindness, generosity, friendliness, and a rich cultural heritage. Some of these friendships were later renewed when some of those we had known in Shanghai came to our capital city as business and diplomatic representatives of their country.

When our academic year at the University had ended, we returned home via Hongkong, Manila, Singapore, Rangoon, Agra, New Delhi, Madras, Cairo, and several cities in Europe. It was in London that I received a letter from the chairman of the pulpit committee of Washington's First Baptist Church inviting me to supply the pulpit there for a

Sunday. The church had been without a pastor for nearly a year and my name was given to the pulpit committee by a friend of mine[1] who had become aware of my interest in international affairs. The one Sunday was followed by other Sundays as guest minister, and ultimately to a call to become pastor.

After a brief vacation, we returned to Washington to take up our duties at the church. While looking for a home, we became temporary residents of the Martinique Hotel, located at Sixteenth and M Streets, Northwest. This hotel was later removed to make way for the erection of the National Education Association's building. A month later, we purchased a residence in the Cleveland Park area of the city, where we lived for thirty-two years. It was while living here that all three of our children were born and where we enjoyed such interesting neighbors as Senator and Mrs. William Proxmire of Wisconsin; Congressman and Mrs. Walter Judd of Minnesota; Undersecretary of Labor and Mrs. Arthur Larson; the military attache of the Chilean embassy; and news commentator Sander Vanocur. Our children had easy access to John Eaton Elementary School, Deal Junior High, and Woodrow Wilson High School. On still days, we could hear the great bells in the tower of Washington Cathedral, several blocks away. Cleveland Park continued to seem like a small-town community even when other areas of the city were undergoing drastic change, and we shall always have a multitude of happy memories related to the years we spent there.

On the day I was to preach my first sermon as pastor of the church—December 6, 1936—the front page of the *Washington Post* was given over largely to a serious crisis in Great Britain—a crisis brought on by the determination of King Edward VIII to marry Mrs. Wallis Simpson, a Baltimore native who had already been divorced twice. Five of the eight columns on the front page of the *Post* that day were filled with stories about the royal romance, and only one of the

1. Dr. Jesse E. Davis of Roanoke, Va.

remaining three columns dealt with the grave illness of Pope Pius XI. One of the stories in the *Post* reported that Prime Minister Stanley Baldwin and Queen Mother Mary were taking a very dim view of Edward's romance, but that a survey of the former Rhodes scholars who were then living in the Washington area revealed that the vast majority of them were altogether on the side of Cupid. I am not at all sure how much of my sermon was absorbed by my congregation that day in view of the sensational things that were taking place in England, but there is no doubt in my mind that my neighbor a block away was receiving the undivided attention of *his* flock. The *Post* reported the next day that he gave Edward and "Wally" quite a going over, denouncing what he called "barnyard morals" at the British court. A few days later, my wife and I sat with others in the parlor of the Martinique Hotel and listened to the radio broadcast of Edward's brief speech of abdication. Following the broadcast, Edward left England for France where he married Mrs. Simpson. More than thirty years transpired before they were received at Buckingham Palace.

My first sermon was entitled "Together We Face the Future," and constituted a blueprint of the matters about which I was primarily concerned and which I intended to stress during my ministry there. In the report of the message which appeared in the *Washington Post* the next day, I find the following sentences:

> Everything about the church should be a demonstration of the vitality, the progressive spirit, and the energetic nature of the mind and message of Christ. I believe not only in the historic facts concerning Christ but also in those things for which he lived and suffered and died. I believe in the abolition of war, the necessity of ridding the world of poverty, in industrial democracy, in Christian cooperation, in international, inter-racial and interdenominational goodwill and understanding, and in the trans-

formation of human character by the impact of the spirit and life of Christ. We face the future together with an unswerving conviction that the cause to which we have given ourselves is destined to succeed. We are in no losing battle.

My installation service was held ten days later, on Wednesday evening, December 16, and, to my delight, was planned to provide for a broad ecumenical representation. Among those participating, and offering words of welcome to the city and to the religious community, were: Bishop William F. McDowell, of the Methodist Church; Dr. Albert J. McCartney, of the Covenant-First (later National) Presbyterian Church; Dr. H. H. Ranck, of Grace Reformed Church; Dr. Carl C. Rasmussen, of the Luther Place Memorial Lutheran Church; Dr. Raphael H. Miller, of the National City Christian Church; Dr. Oliver Hart, of St. John's Episcopal Church (and later Bishop of Pennsylvania); and Dr. Gove G. Johnson, of the National Baptist Memorial Church. Dr. Miller said that serving a Washington church was like trying to preach to a passing train—addressing those in the first coach one Sunday, those in the next coach the following Sunday—but never having the same congregation twice. I was not long in discovering how true these words were. A Washington pastor does not need to move to a new church. If he remains for a while where he is, the new church will come to him. Another friend described his ministry in the capital city as an effort to "evangelize a parade!" While such a situation may appear at first glance to be totally unfortunate, one discovers after a while that even this cloud has a silver lining: one loses not only able leaders but also some who have come to be problems in the life of the congregation!

Government agencies are constantly transferring their employees from one city to another, and many who assume they are settled until retirement keep their psychological bags packed as they anticipate the day when they will "go back home" to the state from which they came. There are also new arrivals each week to replace retirees, and a host of tourists, convention attendants, congressional pages, and other temporary employees of a massive governmental establishment.

One's first reaction borders on despair. He wonders how in the world he is going to create a true spiritual family amidst such chaos, or how he is going to get anything done when someone he has come to depend on in some key leadership position in the church is suddenly picked up and dispatched to San Francisco, London, or Bangkok! However, one soon discovers that newcomers who have had rich experiences in churches elsewhere, bring with them ideas and suggestions which give to a church's program a variety and freshness which prevents a church from getting into a rut or becoming stale. Such new blood also goes a long way toward preventing any one person, or group of persons, from assuming a proprietary attitude toward the church or the direction in which it is going.

Our church was founded in 1802, soon after the national government was moved from Philadelphia to Washington. The community was still small, having a population of approximately six thousand. Thomas Jefferson was president. We were the first Baptist congregation organized in the Washington area, and between that time and the present, hundreds of other congregations have been organized which can trace their ancestry to the old First Church. Luther Rice united with this church when he settled for a while in Washington and during the time he was raising funds for the new mission which he and Adoniram Judson had established in Burma. It was during this time that he founded Columbian College, later to become George Washington University. The first pastor of our church, Obadiah Brown, was the first president of the new college's board of trustees, and rendered great service in helping the young institution to become firmly established. Later in its history, the church sold its edifice at Tenth and E Streets, Northwest, to a Mr. Ford, who remodeled it and turned it into a theater. The theater later burned, was rebuilt, and in this building Mr. Lincoln was shot. With such a long and interesting history, one would suppose that traditional ways of doing things would be impossible to change. Such was not the case. The new life constantly flowing into the congregation gave to the church a youthful spirit which was both stimulating and challenging.

When I began my ministry in Washington, the church occupied a building which was not only strategically located but which, at the time of its construction, must have been a rather imposing edifice. The dark red brick and stone exterior presented a rather somber picture in the winter months, but for most of the year the luxuriant ivy did much to provide a more attractive appearance. The building had been constructed in 1890, and Tiffany had provided the windows as well as the decorations of the sanctuary. The building trades in those days were afraid to dig very far into the ground because of the high water level in the Washington area, and therefore most of the churches erected in Washington at that time had sanctuaries on the second floor above street level. This was true of our church, and anyone who was unable to climb a long flight of stairs was in real difficulty as far as attending church was concerned. I soon gave serious thought to the possibility of launching a building program and began gathering material which would be useful to a future building committee.

When the summer of 1937 arrived, I prepared a proposal to the church regarding the beginning of a process by which we might ultimately construct a new building. Toward the end of July, just before leaving for vacation, I presented the proposal at a meeting of the church on a Wednesday evening. As I look back now, this was a rather presumptuous thing to do since I had been pastor for just over six months. I recall that as I read my recommendations, some of the older members looked both startled and dismayed, and when I concluded my report and sat down, one of the senior officers of the church arose to speak. With great dignity, and with what I interpreted to be a touch of sarcasm in his voice, he made a motion that the whole matter be "referred to a responsible committee of the church." I left for vacation feeling somewhat depressed but determined to take up the matter when the situation seemed more favorable, and my place in the church a little more secure.

During the next two or three years, I occasionally mentioned the proposal for a new and more adequate building, and while the response seemed to be increasing gradually, I was still not entirely sure whether the officials were taking the matter seriously or simply offering what might be considered a courteous encouragement to a young pastor's dreams. It was about this time that I was approached by the pulpit committee of a prominent midwestern church, and decided that this was exactly the time to find out how seriously my hopes for the future of our church were shared by our official family. I, therefore, called together a meeting of all the board and committee chairmen, the church's moderator, and the trustees, and told them frankly about the approach that had been made to me by the midwestern church. I indicated that while the opportunity to be pastor of such a large and aggressive congregation offered numerous advantages to me, I had come to believe so thoroughly in the future of our Washington church that I found it difficult to contemplate leaving. I then shared with them my concern over the extent to which my own ambitions for the church were shared by our official family, and asked that they let me know frankly what their feelings were.

As I recall, each person present assured me of his serious intent to move right ahead with the plans that were necessary for the ultimate construction of an adequate edifice for the expanding program of our congregation, and each pledged his personal support to my leadership in these matters. Within the next few days, the chairman of the Board of Deacons sent a letter to the entire membership of the church, acquainting them with what had taken place, and closed his letter with this paragraph:

In view of our Pastor's great faith in us and our future as a church, I am sure each member will want to share that faith and give to our church and Pastor the most devoted loyalty of which we are capable. We believe that under God's guidance, our church should formulate a progressive program that will prove to be not only a challenge to all our people, but will evoke the interest and admiration of Baptists all over America.

With this assurance, I expressed my deep appreciation to the committee of the church in the midwest for their consideration of me, but declared that my duty to remain with the Washington church and to assist in fulfilling its future plans seemed clear. From that time onward, we moved ahead in implementing some of the proposals which had already been suggested for building the House of God.

Baptist churches in the Washington area operate in a rather unusual fashion. Though confined to one city and its suburbs, these churches formed the District of Columbia Baptist Convention years ago, which functions as a state convention. Feeling that a united denominational witness would be more effective in the nation's capital, this convention became affiliated with both of our national conventions; and while the financial arrangement provided regular budgeted gifts to both the American and the Southern Baptist Conventions, designated gifts to either convention may be made, and each church is free to choose the type of program it finds most helpful to its own particular situation. This makes it possible to serve people from all the states in a unity which recognizes the necessity for diversity, and it would be difficult to find anywhere a finer fellowship among pastors, their wives and their congregations.

II

THE ROOSEVELT ERA

Being invited to the White House, even though you are only one of a large group receiving the invitation, can be quite a significant occasion for a young minister who has recently arrived in Washington, and it certainly was for me. It was the spring of 1938, and President Franklin D. Roosevelt had invited the interdenominational ministers' conference of the city to meet him in his Oval Office. When the appointed day arrived, we gathered first in the auditorium of the Department of Commerce and heard a short address by Secretary Roper, and then walked the short distance to the Executive Mansion. The President remained seated at his desk as we stood around it. His crippled condition was such that standing to his feet or taking a few steps was difficult without assistance.

Dr. Oscar F. Blackwelder, pastor of the Lutheran Church of the Reformation and president of the ministers' conference, had been requested by the conference earlier to seek the help of the president "and other leading men in American life" in an "endeavor to awaken America to the prime importance of restoring moral and spiritual values to their rightful place in the lives of all patriotic citizens." Therefore, in his opening remarks to the president, Dr. Blackwelder said: "We pastors, although holding many different political opinions, wish to pay our respects to you as our fellow churchman as well as Chief Executive. We desire to pledge through you, our thoughts, our prayers, our useful service to our country in these difficult days. No greater thing could come to our land today than a revival of the spirit of religion—a revival that would seep through the homes of the nation and set the hearts of men and women of all faiths to a reassertion of their belief in God, and the dedication of themselves and their world to His will."

In response, Mr. Roosevelt said: "I do not know how you gentlemen feel, but I cannot help feeling myself, from the testimony that comes to me day by day, that there has been a definite and distinct progress toward a spiritual awakening in the last four years. . . . We have made great progress at home and I believe that in making that progress we have had a great influence in other nations of the world. . . . We have gone far . . . toward a greater human security and greater social justice. . . . "

Then the president confessed: "I did not really, deep down in my heart, believe very much in church missions in other lands, but today I do. I have seen what these missions have accomplished in many countries, not only on the religious side but on the side of health and education." This change in view was probably due to the stories which were coming out of China at that time regarding the heroism of certain missionaries who remained at their posts, sharing the dangers and sacrifices of their Chinese friends during the Japanese invasion of that country.

Just as it appeared that our visit to the president was coming to an end, he suddenly picked up a small book which was lying on his desk and explained to us that it was the Book of Discipline of the Methodist Episcopal Church, South. At this time, the union of Methodism in the United States had not taken place. We later learned that the president had received the volume from his press secretary, Steve Early, who was a Southern Methodist and whose pastor, Dr. Albert P. Shirkey, had given the volume to him. Mr. Roosevelt turned to the back section of the book and called our attention to a few pages which were entitled, "The Social Creed of the

Churches." This was a statement setting forth the social implications of the Christian gospel which had been generally accepted by most of the major denominational bodies, and by the Federal Council of the Churches of Christ in the United States. The statement dealt with such matters as the acquisition and use of wealth; a living wage; safeguarding workers from occupational injury; accident and unemployment insurance; shorter working hours; collective bargaining; abolition of child labor; the application of Christian principles to the treatment of offenders; repudiation of war and reduction of armaments; and the rights of free speech, free assembly, and a free press. The president referred to some of these items and then said that if anyone desired a definition of the New Deal, it would be difficult to find a better one than the ideals set forth in this Social Creed of the Churches. While we who stood before him knew that not all Americans would accept this definition of the president's program, or the suggested motivation for it, nevertheless we were convinced that in the president's own mind the New Deal was by no means just a political gimmick to attract voters.

When Mr. Roosevelt was first elected president, he became affiliated with St. Thomas's Episcopal Church, on Eighteenth Street, located at a distance of several blocks from the White House. It was understood that he accepted the position of honorary vestryman there, and while he was not a frequent attendant, the demands of his office and his physical condition made such infrequency understandable. A ramp was installed for his use, but his need for the assistance of others in getting to his feet or walking from one point to another created a spectacle which most persons would prefer to avoid. At Hyde Park, and in a far more private context, Mr. Roosevelt had been a regular attendant at his parish church and had served as a vestryman there. In Washington, he regularly attended the union service on Christmas Day which was sponsored by the Washington Council of Churches. This service alternated from church to church, and representatives of various denominations were called upon to preach. At one of these services, the pastor of the church in which the service was being held was called upon to say a few words regarding a special offering to be taken that day for some urgent, worthy cause. He proceeded to tell the story of the man who was walking through the woods and who was overtaken by a severe storm. In order to find protection from the torrential rain, the man crawled into a hollow log. After a few minutes, the rain ceased and the sun shone brightly. Before the man could crawl out, the log began to shrink and the man found himself trapped. As he lay there, he had plenty of time to think, and his thoughts seemed to concentrate on his past actions which he regretted most. Among these thoughts was the memory of his pitifully small contributions to his church, and within a few minutes he felt so small that he had no difficulty crawling out of the log. As the president threw back his head and laughed heartily along with the rest of the congregation, the pastor concluded: "Now wipe that smile off your face and put in the offering plate the largest bill in your wallet." Reports indicated that the amount received that day was rather impressive.

Mrs. Roosevelt soon became quite a personality in her own right. She gave her support to numerous good causes and unselfishly devoted many hours to luncheons and meetings of various sorts in order that she might lend her personal support to the underprivileged and the forgotten. She went about the city without escort or fanfare and was seen driving her own convertible or shopping at Woodward and Lothrop's store. She soon developed a reputation for being exceedingly resourceful. The newpapers reported that one snowy day in January she stopped by the president's office to bid him goodbye as she was setting out on one of her numerous trips out of town. As she turned to leave, her husband said to her: "Good luck, and if you run into any trouble, telephone me." Mrs. Roosevelt replied: "Thank you, I certainly will, right in the middle of a snow bank!" After she had left the room, the president said to the reporters present, "You know, she just might do that!"

While millions admired Mrs. Roosevelt's spirit and achievements, it was generally recognized that she was not physically beautiful and all sorts of good-natured humorous stories were in circulation about this. One of these had to do with a time when she was supposed to have been at a party where she encountered a man who had obviously partaken of the liquid refreshments too freely. According to the story, he said to the president's wife (not recognizing who she was), "Lady, I believe you are the homeliest woman I have ever seen." After a shocked pause, Mrs. Roosevelt is supposed to have replied: "Well, if I cared to be equally frank, I could say that you are the drunkest man *I* ever saw." The man blinked for a moment and responded: "Yeah, but *I'm* going to be all right tomorrow." Such stories did her no harm for she possessed a beautiful spirit which far more than compensated for any lack of physical attractiveness. Everywhere, she was known as that "gracious lady" whose contributions to her husband's administration, and to her country, were considerable.

It was in these early years of my Washington pastorate that several younger men who had come to the city within a few months of each other began having Friday lunch together. The person primarily responsible for this was an older minister, Dr. William S. Abernethy, pastor for many years of the Calvary Baptist Church. This beloved pastor had had a distinguished career in the nation's capital, serving at one time as president of the Northern Baptist Convention, and being pastor to both President Warren G. Harding and Chief Justice Charles Evans Hughes. Though mature in years, Dr. Abernethy was young at heart, and he took under his wings the younger men who had recently come to the city to serve downtown churches similar to his own. These included Howard Stone Anderson, pastor of the First Congregational Church: Peter Marshall, pastor of the New York Avenue

Presbyterian Church; John W. Rustin, pastor of the Mount Vernon Place Methodist Church; and myself. We met each Friday at the S and W Cafeteria at Fifteenth Street and New York Avenue, and enjoyed visiting together while standing in the cafeteria line, and later at the table. There would be the swapping of humorous stories, the sharing of experiences, an occasional plea for help in the development of some theme for a sermon or illustrations for a specific text, and with it all an unawareness of sectarian traditions and differences. Once a quarter we would have union Sunday evening services with our combined choirs massed together in a group of approximately two hundred voices. We alternated from church to church and took turns with the preaching responsibility. The services were always attended by capacity congregations and the ecumenical spirit became for us not just an idea to be encouraged but an experience to be remembered.

When Peter Marshall died suddenly of a heart attack, his wife, Catherine, asked this group of ministers to take part in the funeral service. We gathered at the appointed time in a room behind the pulpit and were told by the associate pastor the order in which we were to walk onto the pulpit area. He indicated to me that I was to go first. Suddenly I remembered that sometimes as we were standing in the cafeteria line, we would become so absorbed in conversation that the line would move away and leave us, and for some strange reason I would always seem to be the one to notice this, and as a result would become first in line. The others constantly kidded me about this, suggesting that I was so hungry that I could not wait. When the associate pastor instructed me to lead the line of ministers onto the pulpit, I turned to the man behind me and whispered: "I can see Peter now, smiling to himself and saying: 'There goes Ed again, at the head of the line.' " Several weeks later, I met Catherine in the shopping area near our respective homes and told her about this. She was not only amused, but seemed to appreciate the fact that those in the group felt so close together that the barrier which many think exists between time and eternity no longer existed for us. I later discovered that she had related this story in her next book.

From time to time, as members of our group would move to other posts of duty or enter into rest, as was true of Dr. Abernethy and Peter, other ministers would be invited to join us, and among these were Carl Kopf, who succeeded Howard Anderson; Albert P. Shirkey, who succeeded John Rustin; George Docherty, who succeeded Peter; and Clarence Cranford, who succeeded Dr. Abernethy. As with the original group, we continued having occasional union services; would meet regularly for luncheon on Fridays; and meet from time to time on Sunday nights in one another's homes. The latter practice gave our wives an opportunity to become acquainted, and they came to feel as closely knit together as did we. We also had additional contacts in the Interchurch and Theta Sigma clubs for ministers, and in these groups formed lasting ties with numerous other fellow ministers. Among these were Bishop Angus Dun and Dean Francis Sayre, of the Washington Cathedral; Bishops Edwin Holt Hughes and G. Bromley Oxnam, of the Methodist Church; Seth Brooks, of the Universalist National Memorial Church; Albert Joseph McCartney and his successor, Edward L. R. Elson, of the National Presbyterian Church; C. Leslie Glenn, rector of St. John's Episcopal church and later a canon of the Washington Cathedral; Oscar Blackwelder and Gerhardt Lensky, of the Lutheran Church; Frederick E. Reissig, executive secretary of the Washington Council of Churches; and George Davis, of the National City Christian Church. We would meet once a month at four in the afternoon, one of the members would read a paper with general discussion to follow, and we would close with dinner at six. These experiences were tremendously enjoyable and enriching, and produced friendships which have lasted through the years.

One of the most remarkable and inspiring ministers in the city at that time was Dr. Walter H. Brooks who was pastor of the Nineteenth Street Baptist Church for sixty-two years. Born in slavery in Richmond, Virginia, in 1851, Dr. Brooks did not learn to read and write until he was fourteen. He later attended Lincoln University in Pennsylvania, a Presbyterian school, and received his B.A. degree after what he described as "seven long years." Sixty years after his graduation, he sent his alma mater a check for $1,000, in gratitude for what a Baptist pastor had received at a Presbyterian institution. Once, while speaking to a pastors' conference, he said that after he had served the Washington church thirty years, and was sixty-five years old, he got down on his knees and told the Lord he was going to resign and make way for a younger man. He said the Lord then said to him: "What's wrong with my making a young man out of you?" "So," said Dr. Brooks, "I got up and stayed thirty-two years more!" He preached in my pulpit after he was ninety, and his voice was clear and his mind alert. I once greeted him at a reception in honor of Dr. John Compton Ball who had served the Metropolitan Baptist Church for forty years, and suddenly realized that these two men represented over a hundred years of service to the cause of Christ in Washington.

The international crisis, due to Hitler's rise to power in Germany, was becoming more acute day by day, and government personnel began to increase, not only in response to a growing national government, but also in response to certain defense measures which were being put into operation at this time. The city soon became crowded, and it was estimated that between the years 1940 and 1950 the increase in the population of the metropolitan area was the same as though the entire populations of Atlanta and Richmond had moved into Washington and its suburbs. With such a rapid influx of new people, acquiring new members for the church was no problem. One of my fellow ministers said that all one had to do on Sunday mornings was to open the front door of the church and jump back so as not to be run over. It was at this period that several of the downtown churches, including our own, went to two morning services.

The Scott Circle area, in which our church building is located, contained many rooming houses—residences which had once been imposing private homes—and these were filled to overflowing. These people not only *went* to church, but brought their letters of transfer and became active members. For several years, our church received over four hundred new members in each twelve-month period, averaging an increase of more than eight new members each Sunday. When these rooming houses were later replaced by high-rise apartment houses, the situation underwent a drastic change. The rooming house dwellers had been like one big happy family in the commodious residences which they occupied, but the apartment house dwellers, for the most part, desired privacy and wished to be left alone. Later surveys indicated what a vast difference there was between the proportion of rooming house and private residence dwellers who attended church as compared to the proportion of apartment house dwellers who were present at Sunday services.

The churches in the general area of the one I served got together and organized what was called the Massachusetts Mile project. We selected that portion of Massachusetts Avenue nearest the churches involved, and sought by various means to reach the people who lived in the apartment houses in this area. Mailing lists were secured from apartment house managers, and letters and literature were sent. Efforts were made to have church members in these apartments invite their neighbors to tea or have them in for dessert, and have one of the pastors present so that he could get acquainted with some who were not attending church. A retired minister was employed to go from door to door as a representative of all the churches involved and extend an invitation to services, and leave printed materials containing pertinent information regarding the various congregations. Some churches conducted two types of services—a traditional service at eleven in the morning and a contemporary type service on Sunday afternoon. Other churches tried week-night worship services for the convenience of people who were out of the city for the weekend. Few of these efforts were really successful. Either the apartment houses attract a type of individual who does not feel the need for fellowship with other Christians in corporate worship, or else the very nature of apartment houses themselves does something to the person who has formerly felt this need.

It was during Mr. Roosevelt's second term that tensions between our country and Japan began to heighten. The newspapers announced in the summer of 1938 that Japan was sending a new ambassador to the United States—Kensuke Horinouchi. Soon thereafter, I received a letter from a friend who was a missionary in Japan informing me that the new ambassador and his wife were Baptists and members of a small church in the suburbs of Tokyo. My friend indicated that the growing tensions between our two countries would make the ambassador's task all the more difficult, and that any indications of friendship on our part would be greatly appreciated. Since I did not know when the Horinouchis would be arriving in the city, I sent a note to them by mail assuring them of a warm welcome to our church. On their first Sunday in Washington, they were present in our congregation, and at the conclusion of the service, when they had made themselves known to me, I introduced them to a number of our church officials and everyone welcomed them heartily. They continued to attend our services and we came to hold them in high regard. Several months later, when the time arrived for our church's anniversary dinner—the major social event in the church's annual calendar of activities—we invited the ambassador to speak at the dinner, and he readily accepted the invitation. In the course of his address, he referred to the progress which Japan had made over the past eighty years, and added, "I always feel that we are indebted to the American people for much of our progress. Many of Japan's prominent men have been educated or trained in the United States. You have also sent to live among us hundreds of men and women of character and ability, who have in many ways helped our people in every walk of life." Turning then to the presence of American missionaries in Japan, Mr. Horinouchi continued, "They have a high place among those who have

22

served and helped the Japanese people. . . . Not only have they preached the Gospel, but they have also rendered valuable services to the advance of education and medicine in Japan. . . . Today you will find the deep-rooted influence of Christianity in all branches of Japan's cultural life. I would like to take this opportunity to express heartfelt gratitude in the name of the Christians of Japan." Then he spoke with great appreciation of the warmth with which he had been greeted wherever he had been since arriving in the United States; and finally he spoke of his own faith. The following are the two closing paragraphs of his address:

> As a Christian, I was long under a misconception of my religion. To me, it was a beautiful ideal consecrated in a high place quite apart from my daily life. It was something like an angel shut away in a compartment. In days of trouble and hardship, alone I tried to open the doors. I am thankful now that my eyes were opened a few years ago when I first realized that religion should be my daily life. Not only on Sunday, but on every day our life must be God-guided and God-controlled. If we live under the guidance of God, we can live a life of love and unselfishness. I am confident that if everyone sincerely tries to live that kind of life, then, and then only, will all the economic, political, and social problems which trouble us so gravely be capable of solution.
>
> On the eve of our sailing from Japan, an American friend of mine, whose friendship has always been an inexhaustible inspiration to me, gave me a billfold with the inscription: "We are ambassadors therefore on behalf of Christ." It is my hope and prayer that in this inspiration I can serve the cause of bridge-building between America and Japan.

It was not long after this that a letter printed in the *Christian Century* indicated that the ambassador had not received a very cordial reception in Washington and suggested that the churches were probably influenced by the deteriorating relations between Japan and the United States I immediately took this copy of the *Century* to the Japanese embassy and sought an interview with the ambassador. He received me immediately and, after reading the published letter, expressed amazement that anyone could have been so entirely misinformed. He emphasized again how graciously he had been received in the church and elsewhere, and seemed distressed that such an erroneous report had been circulated. I returned to my study and got off an air-mail letter to the editor of the *Century* which was printed in the next issue. However, as is true in so many cases of this kind, I doubt that the correction ever really caught up with the original misinformed report.

After about two years in Washington, the ambassador was called home to Tokyo and replaced by Mr. Nomura who was the Japanese ambassador at the time of Pearl Harbor. I never learned why the change in ambassadors occurred, but could not help but wonder if Mr. Horinouchi's Christian principles made it impossible for him to fulfill his country's requirements of him at a time when conflict between our two nations appeared inevitable. Before leaving Washington, the ambassador and his wife drove to our home and called on us, bringing with them a little teddy bear as a gift for our two-year-old daughter. This gift was enjoyed by all three of our children, and now by our grandchildren. I did not hear from Mr. Horinouchi during the years of World War II, but a year or so after the war had been concluded, he came back to Washington for a visit, and came by my study to see me. When I inquired as to his activities at that time, he replied that he was an instructor in a school for young diplomats in Tokyo, sharing with them his views regarding democratic principles and institutions. As he arose to leave, he told me that I would be receiving by mail soon a piece of pottery produced by one of Japan's foremost artists. This large vase still adorns the pastor's study in the First Baptist Church of Washington.[1]

Among the retired illustrious personalities living in the city at the time was Charles Evans Hughes, former chief justice of the Supreme Court of the United States. Justice Hughes had been governor of the State of New York, the first president of the Northern Baptist Convention, a justice of the U. S. Supreme Court, the Republican candidate for the presidency in 1916 when Woodrow Wilson was running for his second term, and later, chief justice. One day I wrote a note to Justice Hughes indicating how much it would mean to one young Baptist minister to be able to meet one who had occupied such a conspicious place in the life of the denomination, as well as in the life of the nation, and that since my middle name was Hughes, my grandchildren might be puzzled to know how I could have lived in the city with such an illustrious Hughes without having met him! Then I added that if he could spare me a few moments, I would like to stop by his home some day and have the privilege of meeting him. Within a few days, to my surprise, my wife and I received a note from Mrs. Hughes inviting us to tea. Our subsequent visit to Justice and Mrs. Hughes was one of the most memorable experiences of our many years in Washington. They were gracious and warm to a marked degree, and if we entered the home with any tendency to be ill at ease, they caused us to forget this immediately. Justice Hughes told us of his early years in New York City, and of his membership in the Fifth Avenue Baptist Church. He said that at one of the annual meetings of the New York Baptist Association, Dr. McArthur, pastor of the Calvary Baptist Church, took a good-humored sly dig at Dr. Armitage, pastor of the Fifth Avenue Church, saying that the name of Dr. Armitage's church was somewhat misleading since it was not actually located on Fifth

1. On the ambassador's 1974 Christmas card, he wrote that he and his wife had observed the fiftieth anniversary of their wedding and his eighty-eighth birthday during the year.

Avenue. Dr. Armitage got to his feet and replied that while it was true that the Fifth Avenue Church was around the corner from Fifth Avenue, at least they were nearer to Fifth Avenue than Dr. MacArthur's Calvary Church was to Calvary! Fifteen years after our visit to the justice and his wife, and after the justice's death, we chose him to be one of the distinguished members of our denomination to be portrayed in the stained glass windows of the new sanctuary which our church erected.

Within our membership at that time were two aristocratic ladies, Misses Fannie and Lucy Boyce, the daughters of Dr. James P. Boyce, founder and first president of the Southern Baptist Theological Seminary. Dr. Boyce belonged to a wealthy and influential South Carolina family, and, during the early years of the seminary, had assured its continued existence by his own financial support. The commodious apartment in which the Boyce ladies lived seemed almost like a museum with its family portraits, furniture, and silver. Miss Fannie Boyce indicated on one occasion that she would like for me to wear a pulpit robe, saying that her father and other Baptist ministers in the early history of South Carolina were accustomed to wearing robes in Baptist pulpits. This was all the encouragement I needed since I had been wanting to wear a robe for some time. During graduate study days in Scotland, I had preached in a robe on several occasions, and found that it made a definite psychological contribution to the fulfillment of my ministry. John Calvin wore the Geneva gown by way of emphasizing the place of the minister as teacher, and this was his way of rejecting the clerical garments of the Roman Catholic priests. In any case, one Sunday morning I invited into my study the moderator of the Church, the chairman of the Board of Deacons, and the Chairman of the Board of Trustees. I then put on the academic robe I had purchased when I received my doctorate at Edinburgh, and indicated that I would like to wear it in the pulpit that morning. I assured them that I had no desire to create any controversy in the church and would certainly not continue the use of the robe if doing so created any serious problem. They agreed that the congregation would have no basis upon which to base a reaction until they had seen their minister wearing one. No pastor of the church in all of its one hundred fifty years had worn a robe in the pulpit, and many Baptists assumed that robes smacked of Rome and her imitators. In fact, I was so uncertain as to the outcome of the experiment that I did not even tell my wife what I was going to do that morning.

As I walked on to the pulpit, you could have heard a pin drop. I was so self-conscious that at one point in the service I sat when I should have stood, and I found it somewhat disconcerting when I discovered one elderly lady holding her hymnal in front of her face so she would not have to behold such a shocking sight. Soon thereafter, she joined another church. Two couples in the church seemed especially upset by the event, and one of the men came to see me about it. He said that I should discontinue the use of the robe because it was not customary among Baptists. I responded that Baptists had been non-conformists from the beginning and that nothing could be more Baptistic than refusing to be governed by tradition. With these few exceptions, the congregation generally took the whole matter in its stride. I decided to watch the situation carefully and to continue wearing the robe unless there was more evidence that it was hurting the church. One morning, as I was reading the day's mail, I came upon an envelope with the writer's name at the left-hand top corner of the envelope. The name was that of an elderly maiden lady in the congregation whose facial expression usually seemed to reflect displeasure. I immediately thought to myself, "O boy, I'm going to catch it now!" The letter read: "Dear Pastor, I understand that some members of the church are making quite a commotion over your use of a robe in the pulpit. I just want you to know that as long as you continue to preach the Gospel, as far as I am concerned, you can wear a Navajo blanket." With this assurance, I turned my mind to more important matters, and the growth of the church continued without interruption.

One of my University of Shanghai students, Anna May Ing, arrived in Washington with her father, who had been assigned to the Chinese embassy. Within a short time, she got in touch with me and invited me to have a part in her marriage to an outstanding young Chinese, Tennyson Chang. The wedding was held on the lawn of the Chinese embassy with Dr. C. T. Wang, the ambassador, conducting the civil ceremony, and I conducting the religious ceremony. In the years that followed, Dr. Chang taught in several colleges, and he and his family have continued to be among our best friends. Recently, he was able to enter mainland China for a short visit with friends and relatives.

III

THE WAR YEARS

While America's official participation in World War II came suddenly in response to the bombing of Pearl Harbor on December 7, 1941, Washington, in common with most other areas of the nation, had come to feel much earlier that our eventual entry into the war was only a matter of time. When President Roosevelt turned over to the United Kingdom the fifty outdated destroyers following Dunkirk, it was recognized by most Americans that a step had been taken which could be interpreted as a prelude to an eventual declaration of war; and furthermore, there was the general impression that the ships would not be empty when they arrived in the British Isles.

The plight of England following the retreat from Dunkirk has been emphasized by many historians but never more dramatically than by a distinguished British churchman while on a tour of the United States soon after the war ended. Dr. James H. Rushbrooke, president of the Baptist World Alliance, speaking from our pulpit in Washington, said that if he had ever doubted the existence of miracles, his doubts would have been dissolved in the light of what appeared to be three miracles in connection with the Dunkirk experience. He mentioned first the thick cloud cover that enshrouded the English Channel at the time the evacuation of the British forces took place. In such weather conditions, German bombing planes were rendered helpless in their efforts to interfere with the operation. During these fateful hours, as

Dr. Rushbrooke expressed it, "every British citizen who owned a tub, paddled over to Dunkirk and brought some soldier home."

The second miracle, said Dr. Rushbrooke, was the failure of the Germans to follow up Dunkirk with an all-out attack on the British Isles. The British army had found it necessary to abandon all of its equipment on the Continent, and to use Dr. Rushbrooke's words again, "If Hitler's forces had crossed the Channel and attacked England at this time, it would have been an easy conquest, since the British troops did not have even a pop-gun with which to defend themselves."

The third miracle, according to the British visitor, was the sudden cessation of the bombing blitz to which London was subjected. When it seemed that the stricken city would finally be driven to its knees, the bombing abruptly stopped, and there seemed to be no explanation for it. In the light of these observations, one can readily understand how grateful the British leaders were for the fifty outdated destroyers and their cargo.

On Sunday afternoon, December 7, 1941, I was aroused from an afternoon nap by a telephone call from Robert Tate Allen, the editor of religious news for the *Washington Post.* He said he was preparing his column for Monday morning's paper and wanted some quotes from my sermon of that day. I got my notes and gave him a brief summary of what I had said. When we had finished with that, Mr. Allen said rather casually, "We have been getting some rather disturbing reports here at the *Post* that the Japanese may have attacked Pearl Harbor this morning." I replied that this would hardly seem likely since Pearl Harbor was reputed to be the most heavily guarded naval base in the world. However, as soon as our telephone conversation had been concluded, I turned on my radio, and within a few minutes the reports of the bombing were coming in thick and fast.

In the second volume of Cordell Hull's *Memoirs,* the late secretary of State tells of his conversations with Japanese Ambassador Nomura, and the Japanese diplomat, Kurusu, on the day Pearl Harbor was bombed. For months there had been repeated meetings between the representatives of our two governments, reportedly for the purpose of easing tensions and discovering ways to a peaceful solution of existing problems. Mr. Hull had about given up all hope that any further discussions would be useful, and that many of the things he was being told were for the purposes of deception, when the Japanese diplomats insisted on one further meeting on December 7. Mr. Hull reluctantly agreed and the Japanese suggested a time early in the afternoon. While they were waiting in Mr. Hull's outer office, the secretary of State had a telephone call which informed him that the bombing of Pearl Harbor had already taken place. His first impulse was to send the diplomats away without seeing them at all, but on reflection he decided to let them come in and see what they would have to say. When they entered his inner office, they had no idea that he was aware of what had taken place at Pearl Harbor, and very ceremoniously handed him a document purporting to be some new proposal for peace. Mr. Hull, who was thoroughly aroused by this time, took a quick look at the document and then said to his visitors, "I must say that in all my conversations with you during the last nine months, I have never uttered one word of untruth."[1] And then pointing to the deceptive document which had just been handed him, he continued, "In all my years of public service, I have never seen a document that was more crowded with infamous falsehoods and distortions—infamous falsehoods and distortions on a scale so huge that I never imagined until today that any government on this planet was capable of uttering them."[2] Without any further formalities, he showed them the door. Soon thereafter, smoke was seen rising from the back of the Japanese embassy as confidential papers were being burned.

The next morning, we listened by radio to the president's

1. *The Memoirs of Cordell Hull* (New York: Macmillan Co., 1948), Vol. II, p. 1095.
2. Ibid.

message to congress calling for a declaration of war against the Axis powers. The decision of the Congress to comply with the president's recommendation was not long in coming, and within the next few days black-out curtains were installed in the windows of private homes as well as in all public buildings. While the eventuality of war had seemed possible for a long time, the actual attack upon American soil and the swift declaration of war left the residents of Washington stunned and almost unbelieving.

Several weeks before the events at Pearl Harbor took place, I had planned to observe Universal Bible Sunday on December 14, and had asked six persons in our congregation from other countries to participate in the service. I had asked a Japanese, a Chinese, a Russian, a German, an Italian, and a young man from England to sit with me on the pulpit that Sunday, and at the time for the morning's scripture lesson, I wanted each to approach the lectern and read John 3:16 in his own native tongue. They all had agreed. On Monday, following the Pearl Harbor attack, the Japanese girl called me on the telephone and begged to be excused. I thoroughly understood her embarrassment, and while I did not wish to be persistent, I pointed out to her how important it was at that particular time for Christians of all nationalities to bear witness to their oneness in Christ in spite of international crises. After some hesitation, she finally agreed to participate. I knew that the German and the Italian probably had similar misgivings about taking part in such a service, but they did not ask to be excused. On the next Sunday morning, the first Sunday after Pearl harbor, I ascended the pulpit, followed by these nationals from other lands, and it was not difficult to sense the tension in the congregation which the events of the past week had created. When the time came for the scripture lesson, each participant went to the lectern and read the verse from the Gospel of John. As the last reader took his seat, I walked to the lectern and said to the congregation which had been listening with rapt attention, "As we have been reminded again in this portion of God's Word of our Heavenly

Father's great love for us, and of how that love must be reflected in our relationships to one another, let us see to it that no conflict among nations shall ever be allowed to create walls of separation between the followers of Jesus Christ, for Christians are one people." I then suggested that we stand and sing "Blest be the tie that binds our hearts in Christian love," and as we sang, many did so with difficulty as tears coursed down their cheeks. From that day until the end of the war, there seemed to be in the congregation a conscious attempt to place the ties of spiritual unity above any international divisions, and to avoid those unfair generalizations that tend to indict an entire people for what a few leaders have done.

In my preparations for the sermon that day, I had been painfully aware of the highly charged atmosphere in which the message would be delivered. The president had referred to the day of the Pearl Harbor attack as "a day that will live in infamy"; various newscasters had expressed their disgust with what had appeared to be a new low in duplicity on the part of the Japanese diplomats' supposedly seeking peace; and the average man on the street found it difficult to express his resentment with any degree of moderation. What *could* a pastor say of a reconciling nature that would not be interpreted as treason? It was an agonizing experience, and yet I knew that I would probably never again be given such an opportunity to declare what I believed the gospel of Christ had to say to such a crisis in our nation's history. Those to whom I would be speaking would be, for the most part, involved in one way or another in our national government—some of them a part of our military establishment and employed at the Pentagon. Our country had been attacked; our Congress had declared war; already, frantic preparations were underway to increase our defense potential. How could a representative of the Christian faith speak positively to such a complex situation? Everyone was expected to get behind the war effort, and, in a climate of anger and desire for retaliation, there were few indeed who were in the mood for any charitable view of the enemy, or any suggestion that our own hands were not altogether clean.

The message I finally prepared for that first Sunday after Pearl Harbor sought to make the following points: (1) that American Christians were not looking to their churches and their ministers to bless war, or to endorse war, or to promote war, but rather they were saying to their spiritual leaders, "We are *at* war! What does our religion have to offer us at a time like this?" (2) I expressed the conviction that, in such a crisis, God expected us to keep hate out of our hearts. When men are not sure that their cause is just, they seek to bolster their courage through hate, but when they feel justified in defending their country against aggression, they can do so without harboring in their hearts hatred and scorn of those who have offended. There is never a time when an individual must choose between being a good American and a good Christian. (3) I stressed, too, that we lived in a moral universe, and that neither personal nor national sins can be committed without serious consequences. While it is not necessary for us to despise others in order to fulfill our duty toward our country, neither is it necessary to pretend that we are without blame. If we are big enough and brave enough, and our cause is sufficiently just, we can be perfectly honest with ourselves and others. This honesty required of us that we should acknowledge the possibility that some of the scrap iron we had been selling to Japan for use in her aggression against some of her oriental neighbors was used in the creation of the bombs which killed hundreds of our American boys at Pearl Harbor; and that the planes which the invaders used in their attack had probably been powered by gasoline which we had also supplied to them when their military ventures were seemingly being directed against nations other than our own. (4) I sought to underscore the conviction that no international conflicts must ever be permitted to disturb the essential unity of the Christian community throughout the world. The family of Christ transcends all racial, language, and national barriers. (5) Finally, I pointed to the biblical assurances that the ultimate issues of history will not be determined by the schemes and ambitions of men but by the God and Father of our Lord Jesus Christ. "The earth is the Lord's," and "he must reign till he hath put all enemies under his feet." As Martin Luther's great hymn expresses it:

> And though this world, with devils filled,
> Should threaten to undo us,
> We will not fear, for God hath willed
> His truth to triumph through us
>
> Let goods and kindred go,
> This mortal life also;
> The body they may kill;
> God's truth abideth still,
> His kingdom is forever.

Two weeks after Pearl Harbor, Prime Minister Winston Churchill came to Washington to confer with President Roosevelt on the conduct of the war. His visit extended over Christmas Day, and, as stated in the previous chapter, Mr. Roosevelt always attended the union Christmas service which was sponsored by the Washington Council of Churches. The service that year was held in the Foundry Methodist Church on Sixteenth Street, just a block from my own, and the preacher was the Rev. Zebarney Phillips, rector of Epiphany Episcopal Church. When it became known that both the president and the prime minister would be present, we were not surprised to learn that extreme security measures would be used to guarantee the personal safety of the two most powerful figures in the Allied world. A limited number of tickets were issued to the cooperating congregations, and the pastor issuing these tickets was responsible for the person to whom the ticket was given. As we approached the church that morning, the building looked like an armed fortress. Marines, armed with rifles, were stationed around the church, at its doors and on the roof. As I sat with other clergy in the chancel during the service, I looked up into the organ chambers and noticed marines there also, with rifles drawn. It was a strange setting for a Christmas service, and seemed hardly the place for the emphasis in song and sermon of "Peace on earth to men of goodwill." Both the president and the prime minister participated in the hymns and the responsive reading, and listened intently to the Christmas message contained in the sermon. It was a memorable occasion, but everyone present breathed a sigh of relief when it was all over and nothing had happened to endanger the lives of those present.

After the war had been in progress for two years, I was asked by the *Washington Evening Star* to write a column to be entitled, "The Mission of the Church." At that time, there was a wide variety of opinion as to the role of the church in a nation at war, and some denominational bodies had passed through some unpleasant experiences as the issue was debated at annual meetings. A prominent minister of my own communion had sought to get the annual convention to go on record as "supporting the war effort." This attempt was met with vigorous debate and the proposal was defeated. However, such encounters left some sore spots in personal relations that did not heal quickly. The matter I was asked to write about, then, was no academic matter, but one about which there was serious disagreement. After referring to the differing points of view on the subject, I wrote:

> It is my conviction that the role of the church in wartime is the role of the church at any time, and that is a spiritual role. If there is ever a time when the spiritual ministry of the church is needed, it is in a time of war; and we render ourselves rather ineffective when we forget that fact and concern ourselves with the material resources of our fighting machine. There are a thousand and one organizations seeking to increase our military strength, while the Church is the only institution dedicated to the task of increasing America's spiritual strength; and to my mind, the

church is making a tragic mistake when it becomes so engrossed in the material phases of waging a war that it neglects this indispensable ministry. . . . If history teaches anything at all, it is what the writer of Ecclesiastes expressed when he wrote: "The race is not to the swift, nor the battle to the strong." Might does not make right, and God is not always on the side with the strongest army. . . . The greatest guarantee of a nation's survival is not in its tanks and guns, but in the quality of its soul. The Psalmist gave expression to this conviction when he wrote: "Some trust in chariots, and some in horses; but we will remember the name of the Lord our God." . . . If the Church is to fulfill its divinely appointed mission, it must produce and maintain men and women of large spiritual stature, for with them rests the hope of the world.

As the war continued, it became obvious to everyone that the only hope the Allied forces had for survival was a return to the Continent. During the early months of 1944, there was much speculation as to the probable date of an Allied landing in Europe and just where the landing would be made. There were frequent reports in the press which indicated that troops and equipment were being accumulated in the British Isles in large quantities, and that the landing in Europe, whenever and wherever it came, would be a costly venture. Churches were alerted to be ready to open their doors for prayer and meditation on the day the crossing took place. One night in June of that year, I drove out to Silver Spring, one of the suburban areas of Washington, to call on an elderly member of our church. When the visit was over, and I arose to leave, the lady and her daughter walked with me out of the house, and we stood talking for a few moments in the bright light of a beautiful full moon. As I said good night to the ladies, I added, "This would make an ideal night for a landing in Europe." The next morning the radio announced that a landing had indeed been made that night on the Normandy beaches, and that the operation had begun about the time I had made the remark. While the loss of life and equipment was great during those first invasion hours, reports indicated that a firm foothold had been achieved and that probing actions were already in progress in the nearby countryside and villages. Since many in the Washington churches had relatives among the servicemen involved, relief that a successful landing had finally been made was tempered by tremendous anxiety and distress over the price at which the feat had been accomplished.

President Roosevelt's health became a topic of widespread concern as his campaign for a fourth term was being waged that fall. On one campaign trip to New England, he seemed to be making an effort to prove the satisfactory condition of his health by riding, bareheaded, in an open car while a cold rain was falling. However, pictures of him at that time clearly showed that he was feeling the strain of his twelve years in office and the heavy responsibilities of the war in Europe and the Far East. In December, following his election, he travelled to Yalta for a summit conference and, returning home at Christmas time, he went to his home at Hyde Park to rest from his exhausting trip. This meant, of course, that he would miss the union Christmas service which he regularly attended.

The Christmas service that year was to be held at the Washington Cathedral, and I had been chosen to preach the sermon. In the congregation were Vice President and Mrs. Henry A. Wallace, Secretary of the Navy and Mrs. Frank Knox, and other dignitaries. My topic that morning was "The Spiritual Basis for Peace," and expressed the hope that we would not make

> the mistake of believing that world peace is something for which world statesmen are alone responsible. While we are profoundly grateful for the progress toward world peace which may have been made at the recent conferences in Moscow, Cairo, and Teheran,

we must recognize very frankly that conferences, treaties, and military victories can result only in rearranging men as they are, and men can be disarranged just as easily as they can be rearranged . . . We owe it to our national leaders to implement their statesmanship with those personal attitudes which made agreements among men workable.

Early in April, 1945, the president went to Warm Springs, Georgia, for a period of rest. On the night of April 15, the building committee of our church had a dinner meeting at the Iron Gate Inn on N Street. One of the committee members, who was treasurer of the World Bank, arrived late and, since we were already eating and in the midst of a discussion of some phase of the building program with the architect who had come down from Philadelphia, the latecomer ate his dinner silently. When all of us had finished eating and were preparing to leave the table, the member who had arrived late told us that before leaving his office, he had been informed that the president had died that afternoon of a cerebral hemorrhage. We had planned to return to the church following the dinner for an extended discussion of matters pertaining to the proposed new building, but now were in such a state of shock and distress that we rather hurriedly reached agreement on a few matters about which the architect needed immediate information, and adjourned. Little did we realize that night that the new president, sworn in that afternoon, was destined to play such an interesting role in the history of our church for the next several years.

IV

MR. TRUMAN COMES TO CHURCH

When, in 1944, Senator Harry S. Truman of Missouri was elected to serve as vice president of the United States in President Roosevelt's fourth term as chief executive, the moderator of our congregation, Mr. Elgin Smith, and I wrote to him and asked for an appointment. He consented to see us and suggested a time for our visit. On the appointed day we went to the Capitol and were directed to his office. Both of us were surprised at the small and inconspicuous quarters which had been assigned to the vice president, but now in retrospect I recall that the dynamic Mr. Roosevelt seldom gave the impression that he was delegating to his vice president any major responsibilities. John Nance Garner, who had also served as Mr. Roosevelt's vice president, once described the office he held in rather uncomplimentary terms, and Mr. Truman, after succeeding to the presidency, confided in his friends that he had had little significant preparation for the awesome responsibilities which fell upon his shoulders when Mr. Roosevelt died. Our visit to Vice President Truman that day was very pleasant. We immediately sensed his warm and friendly personality and were made to feel completely at ease. We told him that we had come to invite him to attend First Baptist Church and assured him that we would do everything possible to make his visits as normal as possible. He thanked us cordially and expressed the hope that his duties would permit him to visit us soon. Only a few months intervened between our visit to Mr. Truman and Mr. Roosevelt's death, and if Mr. Truman attended our church during that time, we were not aware of it.

Soon after Mr. Truman became president, our church office received a call from a representative of *Time* and *Life* magazines saying that he had interviewed the new president and had learned that he attended our church. He then indicated that he would like to speak to someone who might provide some information as to the president's church-going habits. We were embarrassed because we had no knowledge of his attendance, though we certainly could not deny it. The vice president had not been a conspicuous figure, and it is entirely possible that he had attended our church either as senator or vice president without our learning of it. In any case, we composed a letter of invitation to the new president, signed by the principal officers of the church and myself, assuring him of a warm welcome to our congregation, and indicating that we would make arrangements for his attendance according to his desires, providing him with a private entrance to the building if he preferred one. He responded with a note of thanks and indicated that he hoped to be able to attend at some time in the future. The response was so indefinite that we really didn't know whether he would ever come or not.

One Saturday night in October, 1945, six months after Mr. Truman had become president, my home telephone rang and, while the caller gave me his name, I had not the slightest idea who he was. He said that he would like to come out to my home and see me for a little while. Not knowing who he was, or what he wanted, I explained that it was a difficult time for me to see anyone since my wife was out of the city with her mother who was ill, and that I had given our two small children their dinner and was getting ready to put them to bed. I also pointed out that I still had some work to do on my sermon for the next day, and asked if he could possibly see me after church the next morning. He replied that this would not do. He then identified himself as a member of the Secret

Service and said he wanted to see me about the president's visit to our church the next morning. He said that he and some of his associates had already been to the church and decided where and when the president should enter the building, but that he would like to go over some details with me. I responded by saying that under the circumstances I thought he had better come on out! It is needless to say that by the time I had concluded the conversation with the Secret Service man, there was no time left for any substantial changes in the sermon I was preparing for the next morning, but since I had already announced my topic, "A Time for Greatness," I decided that this subject was not wholly inappropriate for a president of the United States who was facing one of the most exacting periods in our entire history as a nation.

The president had chosen to attend our early service at 9:30 A.M. which was more of a family service and less crowded than the one at 11, and since our church was not far from the White House, he walked the distance, accompanied by one or two Secret Service men. Other members of the Secret Service were scattered through the congregation, though this was not known to those present. In the announcement period, I acknowledged the presence of the president and extended a brief but cordial welcome. On his subsequent visits, I did not refer to him at all.

My text that morning was John 12:27: "Now is my soul troubled and what shall I say? Father, *save* me from this hour? But for this cause came I to this hour. Father, glorify thy name." The introduction of the sermon was as follows:

> As we view the world scene around us today, we are reminded of the words of the poet, Arthur C. Coxe, "We are living, we are dwelling, in a grand and awful time." But the poet was a man of faith and, refusing to be alarmed at what he saw, he continued his lines in a spirit of courage and confidence, when he added: "In an age on ages telling, to be living is sublime."

Someone tells the story of an elderly Scottish highlander who went to church one night and heard a sermon on the greatness and expansiveness of the universe. The minister had a great deal to say about the tremendous distances between the various stars and planets. The old man was momentarily stunned and depressed by what he had heard, and as soon as the service was over, he went out into the darkness and stood alone for quite a while looking at the stars. A little later, as someone passed near him, the old man was heard to say to himself: "I refuse to be astronomically intimidated." And so the *poet* refused to be intimidated by the awe-inspiring nature of the time in which he lived. Instead of trying to run away from it all, he chose rather to believe that "to be living is sublime."

I then referred to some of the major events of that year, 1945: the conquest of Italy; the overthrow of Nazi Germany; the defeat of Japan; the emergence of Russia as a world power; the ascent of China to first place among Oriental nations; and the disclosure of the means by which atomic power could be harnessed and used; and then suggested that 1945 might well go down in history as the year in which more gigantic events took place than in any other year in recorded history. This recital of the unprecedented combination of developments within the span of a single year, prompted the following question:

> And how shall we react to it? For guidance concerning this, we turn instinctively to Him whose name we bear, for He, too, lived in "a grand and awful time." When only thirty-three years of age, He felt the pressure of growing opposition, and knew that His cruel death could not be far away. It was in that hour that He said: "Now is my soul troubled; and what shall I say? Father, *save* me from this hour? But for

this cause came I to this hour. Father, glorify Thy name." Here is every evidence of a great struggle. On the one hand was the normal impulse to run away from it all; and on the other was a sense of destiny which he could not ignore. We know the outcome of that gigantic struggle. What then shall be the Christian's response to the challenge of grand and awful days? "Father, save us from this hour?" No, for it was for this very hour that we were born.

At this point I suggested that our critical time in history called for the same qualities of character which were to be found in the life and ministry of Jesus as he faced his hours of crisis: faith, courage, sympathy and understanding, consecration and sacrifice. Then I undertook to interpret each of these qualities of character in its particular relevance to the circumstances of our time: seeing faith as a commitment to pioneering and action rather than an unquestioning acceptance of ancient dogmas or the espousal of time-honored institutions; seeing courage as a willingness to forfeit one's natural desire for approval and devoting one's self to unpopular causes, and becoming the champion of the despised and the ignored; seeing sympathy and understanding as positive contributions to international concord in addition to their improvement of personal relationships; seeing consecration as the acceptance of all the pain and frustration which is invariably the lot of those who become involved in the sufferings of mankind; and seeing sacrifice as the only way of life for those who cast in their lot with Him who "steadfastly set his face to go to Jerusalem." This was followed by this concluding paragraph:

> We shall never make our supreme contribution to the world as a nation until we learn the art of sacrifice. We must learn to sacrifice our pride and prejudices; our sense of superiority over other peoples; our narrow nationalism and individualism; our self-

centeredness and our preoccupation with merely local interests. The world will never be on the road to permanent peace until we are willing to sacrifice for peace as much as we have been willing to sacrifice for war. We need to remember that Jesus became the world's Savior, not by conquering the world, nor by subduing the world, nor by coercing the world, but by dying *for* the world.[1]

At the close of the service, in accordance with a long-established custom, I asked the congregation to be seated following the benediction, and to remain seated until the president and his party had left the sanctuary. I then walked down to the president's pew and accompanied him out of the building to the street where his car was waiting. He was gracious in his reactions to the service, and again gave me the impression of being a very cordial and friendly individual. We must have complied with his wishes concerning the manner in which he wished to be treated since he continued to attend our services for the next several years as his schedule would permit. In an item from the president's diary printed in the book, *Mr. President*, Mr. Truman wrote:

> I go for a walk and to church. The preacher always treats me as a church member and not the head of a circus. That is the reason I go to the First Baptist Church.[2]

He made a similar statement to a group of Protestant editors who called on him at the White House. I accompanied members of the Associated Church Press on their visit to the president, and presented them to him. After thanking me, he said that he hoped he was more of a credit to the church than a liability and referred to the burdens of his office which prevented him from attending regularly. Then he added that

1. Edward Hughes Pruden, *Interpreters Needed* Philadelphia: Judson Press, 1951. Reprinted by permission of the publisher.
2. William Hillman, *Mr. President* (New York: Farrar, Strauss and Young, 1952) p. 134.

when he did attend church, he was treated exactly as he wanted to be treated. He concluded his remarks by saying that he attended church "not for the purpose of making a show, but because I want to go and think I ought to go."

A few weeks after Mr. Truman's inauguration in 1949, my friend, Congressman Brooks Hays, wrote me a letter in which he said:

> A few days ago I had a delightful visit with President Truman and in the course of the conversation your name was mentioned. I know you would have been pleased with his comments about you and the First Church. It should give you keen satisfaction to know how grateful he is for the understanding and sympathetic handling of his relationship to the church and the provision you make for his spiritual refreshment . . . He spoke with obvious appreciation of your refusal to capitalize on his attendance at First Church.

In a letter to me, Mr. Truman once wrote:

> I get a lot of pleasure out of coming to church. I don't want you ever to feel that you are in any way handicapped in your freedom of speech and expression just because I happen to be there. I want to be treated like every other citizen and every other good Baptist. One of the things I am one hundred per cent for is freedom of expression as long as it is within the bounds of reason and decency.

One Sunday, following the president's attendance at church, those who counted the offering found a five-dollar bill with a note pinned to it. The note was written on White House stationery, and the bill had been autographed by Mr. Truman. The note read: "The deacon who counts this one may have it for a keepsake provided he puts two like it in its place." Since we were in the midst of a strenuous building fund campaign at that time, I was tempted to get the president to autograph several thousand-dollar bills and then to auction them off to the highest bidder!

On another Sunday, our church telephone rang and one of the church officials who happened to be in the church office answered it. A spokesman at the White House said that he was calling to let us know that the president had left the White House and was walking to church. The church official responded by saying that the early service that day would be largely a service of promotion for Sunday School children who would be moving from one age group to another, and that he was afraid this would not be of much interest to the president. The White House spokesman replied by saying that it was too late to inform the president of this since he was probably approaching the church at that very minute. I was immediately notified of this conversation and must confess that I was disturbed since I naturally wanted the service to be especially helpful to the president when he attended. I then did what I had not done before—I went to the front door of the church to meet the president when he arrived so that I could explain the circumstances to him. When he entered the vestibule and we had shaken hands, I explained somewhat apologetically the type of service we had planned for the early service, and frankly would not have been surprised if he had thanked me and said he would come back another day. Instead, he assured me that this would not disturb him in the least, and furthermore that he was fond of children and would enjoy the proceedings. Then, on the spur of the moment, and without any previous thought whatever, I asked him if he would say a few words to the children after they had received their certificates of promotion. He readily agreed to do so, and at the appropriate place in the service I announced to the children that their commencement speaker would be America's first citizen, the president of the United States. Mr. Truman arose from his pew, walked down the aisle, and took his stand in front of the communion table. He then spoke to the children for several minutes about how fortunate they were to be able to grow up in a democracy where the principles of the Christian faith were known and taught, and where each person could worship God according to the dictates of his own heart. Needless to say, both the children and their parents were tremendously pleased. The next day *The New York Times* (September 29, 1947) published a news story concerning the president's visit to church under the headline: "Truman at Church: Talks to Children." Then, on its editorial page, printed the following editorial:

Dr. Pruden's Parishioner

Democracy is hard to define, though many gifted persons have tried to find the words. Longitude in these days also makes a difference. But possibly in a democracy something like this might happen: The head of the State, facing a series of painfully difficult and unspeakably important decisions, might wish to go to church. He might leave his front door, accompanied by a single secret service man, and walk the eight blocks, without any parade or crowds, but possibly with a few fellow-citizens tipping their hats to him. When he got to church the minister might ask him to say a few things to the Sunday School Children, who were about to receive their "Rally Day" certificate of promotion. He might oblige, in simple and not necessarily original language, because, as he would put it, he was "crazy about children." Then he might listen while the pastor preached a sermon on faith. He might think he needed faith at this time. After the sermon he might shake hands with the pastor and a few others and walk back home to lunch—or maybe, as country-bred folks often do, he might call the midday meal dinner.

An incident like this would not prove that the country in which it occurred was a perfect democracy. But it would be the sort of thing that could happen in a not too perfect democracy, in which the head of the State is a servant of the people and sometimes doubts his own unaided strength to bear the burden placed upon him. Americans of all faiths will like to know that this is the way it was when Harry S. Truman dropped into the First Baptist Church in Washington yesterday and heard a sermon by Dr. Edward Hughes Pruden.

So, after an official of the church, and the pastor, had tried to warn the president concerning a service in which he might not be interested, that very service turned out to be the most memorable of all those which Mr. Truman attended at our church.

Bill Henry, a Baptist minister's son, an associate teacher of one of our Sunday School classes, and the Washington correspondent for the *Los Angeles Times,* was present one morning when the president was in attendance. The column he supplied for his paper on Tuesday, February 1, 1949, was entitled, "The President Goes to Church." The following are excerpts from that column:

> *WASHINGTON*—It was wintry on Sunday morning all right. You could feel it right through your ribs when you walked the mile or so to the early service. You went up the stairs and had to look pretty carefully before you saw him seated there, two-thirds of the way back, right in the middle of other worshippers with another Secret Service man beside him and, over at the other end of the pew, a girl who, if she was aware that she was sharing the bench with the President of the United States, didn't betray it in any way.
> *SERVICE*—The President isn't perfunctory about his worship. He wears his serious expression, which can be pretty grim, and he listens intently. He grabs for the hymnal and rifles through the pages to

the right number and is among the first to his feet when it's time to stand up, sharing the hymn book with the Secret Service man. Neither of them do much singing but they join in the responsive reading, and the President got a bang out of the children's sermon, which was about the little boy with the loaves and fishes.

SERMON—And the sermon for the grown folks was about "Christian Mysteries" and Dr. Pruden told how we all love mysteries, even to the point of trying to make mysteries where none exists. He told how at the inauguration the reporters had tried to make a mystery out of the delay between the appointed hour of noon and the time when the ceremony actually began. And he said the reporters had checked with him, because he had opened the inaugural with an invocation, and he said he would have liked to have made them happy by telling them that the President had forgotten his speech or something equally interesting but the real truth was that there wasn't any mystery at all—it just took that long for all those people to find their places on the platform.

LESSON—The President smiled at that! And Dr. Pruden went on to say that religion is like that, too. Some people try to make a mystery of it but actually this is a practical, matter-of-fact world, and religion, to help us meet the world's problems, must be practical and matter-of-fact too, otherwise it can't be of much assistance. . . . And when the service was about over, he asked everybody to remain seated until the President had left, and they walked out together—just the two of them and the one Secret Service man—and you remembered church services in other countries where the presence of the first citizen meant soldiers and police and a great to-do, and you thought it was rather nice to live in a country where the Chief Executive's worship is taken as a matter of course.

I learned from some source that there was a special prayer which the president had used at various times in his life, and I asked him on one of my visits to the White House to let me have a copy of it. He wrote it out in his own hand, and it is as follows:

> Oh! Almighty and Everlasting God, Creator of Heaven, Earth and the Universe:
>
> Help me to think, to act what is right; make me truthful, honest and honorable in all things; make me intellectually honest for the sake of right and honor and without thought of reward to me. Give me the ability to be charitable, forgiving, and patient with my fellowmen—help me to understand their motives and their shorcomings—even as Thou understandest mine!
>
> Amen, Amen, Amen.[1]

He once declared that this prayer had been used by him

> from high school days, as window washer, bottle duster, floor scrubber in an Independence, Missouri, drugstore, as a timekeeper on a railroad contract gang, as an employee of a newspaper, as a bank clerk, as a farmer riding a gang plow behind four horses and mules, as a fraternity official learning to say nothing at all if good could not be said of a man, as a public official judging the weaknesses and shortcomings of constituents, and as President of the United States of America.[2]

I can honestly say that, in all my contacts with Mr. Truman, it seemed to me that his prayer had had a tremendous influence upon his life. The characteristics of the man which impressed me again and again were those for which he had prayed so often.

1. William Hillman, *Mr. President* (New York: Farrar, Straus and Young, 1952), introductory section.
2. *Ibid.*

Dr. Pruden giving the invocation at the inauguration of President Truman. From left to right: President Truman; Sam Rayburn, Speaker of the House; Chief Justice Frederick M. Vinson; Dr. Pruden; and Vice President Alben Barkley.

Wide World Photos, Inc.

President Truman talking to three ministers following his address to the Washington Pilgrimage Convocation. Left to right: Dr. Ralph W. Sockman. pastor of Christ Church (Methodist). New York City; Dr. Warren Hastings, pastor of National City Christian Church. Washington; and Dr. Pruden.

Wide World Photos, Inc.

President Truman, Mrs. Truman and Margaret, leaving church with Dr. Pruden on Thanksgiving Day, 1946.

Associated Press Photo

President Eisenhower with other participants in a Prayer Breakfast held at the Mayflower Hotel in Washington. Left to right: Abraham Vereide, Prayer Breakfast chairman; Congresswoman Frances Bolton of Ohio; President Eisenhower; Senator Frank Carlson of Kansas; Conrad Hilton, hotel executive; and Dr. Pruden.

President Kennedy greeting guests at a reception in the White House following a swearing-in ceremony for Hon. Brooks Hays. Left to right: Vice-President Lyndon Johnson; President Kennedy; former Secretary of the Interior, Oscar L. Chapman; Dr. Pruden; Peace Corps Director Paul Geren; and Dr. Clarence W. Cranford. Mr. Hays' pastor.

Abbie Rowe

Dr. and Mrs. Pruden with pages at a gala reception celebrating their twenty-five years at First Baptist Church, Washington.

Curtis Richel

The Pruden family with Chief Justice and Mrs. Warren at the twenty-fifth anniversary reception. Left to right: Edward H. Pruden, Jr.; Dr. Pruden; Mrs. Pruden; Mrs. Warren; Chief Justice Warren; Patricia Pruden Partridge (the Prudens' daughter); and William Partridge.

Curtis Richel

Dr. Pruden with guests at one of the anniversary dinners at First Baptist Church. Left to right: Dr. Pruden; Chief Justice Earl Warren; Secretary of the Treasury, Robert Anderson; and Speaker of the House of Representatives, Sam Rayburn.

Muse Photo Bureau

President Lyndon B. Johnson leaving First Baptist Church with Dr. Pruden. The president is holding the little son of Postmaster General Marvin Watson, and Edward H. Pruden, Jr. is in the background.

Wide World Photos, Inc.

The sanctuary of the First Baptist Church in Washington.

Curtis Richel

V

MEMORIES OF THE PRESIDENT

One could not be with Mr. Truman very long without feeling the warmth of his personality and his unfailing thoughtfulness. He had a way of putting his visitors immediately at ease, and the sincerity of his manner came through in an unforgettable way. When people would ask me what kind of person I found him to be, I could think of nothing more expressive of my own reactions to the man than to say that he was the kind of person anyone would like to have for a next-door neighbor. One sensed a complete absence of pretense; there was no effort to impress; and while his expressions of concern or approval were always restrained, one felt that they were entirely genuine and that the person to whom he was talking really meant something to him. The first time my wife met him, she said, "That isn't the man I've heard on the radio and seen on television. In some way the electronic media fails to capture the warmth and strength of the man. All he needs to do to be elected in the next campaign is to meet a sufficient number of people." And, of course, that is exactly what he did. His whistle-stop tour across the country in 1948 brought him face to face with hundreds of thousands who, for the first time, saw him as he really was.

It was not uncommon to hear the president call to one of the Secret Service men and inquire about an ill daughter, or a wife who was in the hospital. Once, when my mother was visiting me in Washington, I took her to see Mr. Truman in his office in the White House. In the months that followed, almost without exception, when he would see me he would ask, "How is your mother?" Everyone knew of his devotion to his own mother and how frequently he visited her in Grandview, Missouri. One spring during the period Mr. Truman was attending our church, I let the president know that we were planning to place special flowers on the communion table on Mother's Day in honor of his mother. Immediately there came a note from the president saying how much he appreciated this and that he would like to supply the flowers from the White House green houses. In ample time for the service, we received a magnificent basket of spring flowers which contributed a great deal to the meaning of the occasion for us all.

Once, with great amusement, Mr. Truman told me what an unreconstructed Confederate his mother was. He said that as she prepared to come to Washington to visit him at the White House, his brother, Vivian, said to her: "Mama, suppose Harry makes you sleep in President Lincoln's bedroom." With genuine determination in her voice, she replied, "If Harry puts me in that room, I'll sleep on the floor before I'll sleep in Abe Lincoln's bed."

President and Mrs. Truman were in church on the first Sunday in December, 1946, which was the beginning of the church's celebration of my tenth anniversary as pastor. The anniversary committee had prepared a booklet for the occasion which listed the various features of the observance and these were given out at the service that morning since it included the order of service for the day. Evidently the president noted that there would be a reception on Wednesday evening because there arrived at the church Wednesday afternoon a box of beautiful flowers with a card of congratulations from the president and Mrs. Truman.

Mrs. Truman and their daughter, Margaret, were members of the Episcopal Church, but occasionally accompanied the president to services in our church. The president's informal and homey way of doing things was illustrated on the first Sunday Mrs. Truman accompanied him to our service. Following our usual custom when Mr. Truman was present, I pronounced the benediction and, while the congregation remained seated, I left the pulpit and walked down the aisle toward the president's pew. President and Mrs. Truman stepped out into the aisle and, just before I reached them, Mrs. Truman started toward the door, assuming, I am sure, that the president would introduce me to her after we had reached the vestibule. As soon as Mr. Truman saw what was happening, he called out in a stage whisper, "Bess! Bess!" and gestured with his right hand for her to turn around and come back. Mrs. Truman responded, and with the entire congregation looking on, we were introduced. Then the three of us walked out of the church to the street where the White House limousine was waiting. Occasionally the president accompanied Mrs. Truman and Margaret to St. John's Episcopal Church on Lafayette Square, especially at Christmas and Easter when St. John's would have a service even earlier than our early service, and then the three of them would come together to our service later.

Both Mrs. Truman and Margaret were always gracious in every way, and it was evident to everyone that a happy family relationship existed between the president and his wife and daughter. Occasionally I commented to friends that the president's daughter, constantly in the limelight, must have had numerous opportunities to say or do something that might be an embarrassment to her parents, but she never did. The impression she made on those who had any opportunity to observe her was that she was a very wholesome and attractive young lady. When she graduated from George Washington University, the ceremonies were held in Constitution Hall. Her father gave the commencement address and I gave the invocation. In the waiting room just off-stage where we waited prior to the beginning of the ceremonies, I reminded the president of the close relationship our church had had in the founding and early years of the college out of which George Washington University grew, and he seemed particularly pleased to know of this.

I visited Mr. Truman occasionally in his Oval Office at the White House, and one of these visits was on the day that the *Washington Post* published a story regarding our proposed new church building, including a picture of the architect's drawing. After we had talked a few minutes about other matters, the president wheeled around in his desk chair and picked up a copy of the *Post* which was on the table behind him. He expressed interest in the project and generally praised the architect's design. Then he said that he was somewhat of an amateur architect, having made something of a study of cathedrals he had seen in Europe, and that his only disagreement with our architect was regarding the size of the steeple over the main entrance. He thought it was not in keeping with the massive size of the edifice itself. As it happened, the drawing had been made by an elderly member of the architectural firm who by this time had retired, and when I related Mr. Truman's comments to the younger architect who took over the firm, he said that the president was right, and that he would be making a new drawing of the building with a substantial tower replacing the rather slender steeple.

On another visit to the White House, while waiting to see the president, I fell into conversation with a member of the White House staff. When I mentioned to him my impression of the president as one possessing a warm and pleasant personality, this staff official—a man of husky physical appearance, responded by saying, "I know it is an odd term to apply to a man, but I can think of no better way to describe him than to say that he is really a *sweet* man. We who work here love to be around him." These occasional White House visits also included a tea which my wife and I attended at the invitation of Mrs. Truman.

On rare occasions, Mr. Truman attended week-night meetings in connection with some unusual event of religious significance. One such occasion was a service in our church in recognition of the establishment in Washington of the headquarters of the Baptist World Alliance. Formerly the headquarters had been located in London, but it was ultimately recognized that since such a large proportion of the Baptist population of the world resided in the United States, the program of the Alliance could best be conducted from a Washington office. When I learned that the president would attend, I arranged to meet him upon his arrival. As his car rolled up in front of the church, a Secret Service man who had arrived ahead of the car opened the car door. It was a cold night and the president was wearing an overcoat. As soon as he stepped out of the car, he removed his overcoat and handed it to the Secret Service man, saying: "Keep a close watch on this coat tonight. There are lots of Baptists around!" We went into the lower hall of the church for a brief reception, during which time I had the privilege of presenting the leaders of our denomination from around the world to the president, among them being the president of the Alliance, Dr. C. Oscar Johnson, a fellow Missourian with whom he was already acquainted. Later we went to the sanctuary for the program of the evening and Mr. Truman extended to the visitors from abroad a warm welcome to Washington.

Another of these special occasions was an annual meeting of the Washington Pilgrimage, an organization established for the purpose of stressing our country's spiritual heritage. Mr. Truman agreed to speak at a night session of the pilgrimage which was held at the National City Christian Church, the church which President Lyndon Johnson attended during his administration. Appearing with the president on the program was Dr. Ralph Sockman of New York City; Dr. Warren Hastings, pastor of the host church; and I presented the president when the time arrived for him to speak. Included in his brief address are these lines:

> You will see as you make your rounds, that this nation was established by men who believed in God. You will see that our founding fathers believed that God

created this nation. And I believe it, too. They believed that God was our strength in time of peril and the source of our blessings. You will see the evidence of this deep religious faith on every hand. . . . To our forefathers, it seemed something of a miracle that this nation was able to go through the agonies of the American Revolution and emerge triumphant. They saw, in our successful struggle for independence, the working of God's hand. . . . - Millions of Americans since then have believed that the keeping of our Republic depends upon keeping the deep religious convictions on which it was founded. From the worship and teachings of the synagogues and churches of our land, have come a moral integrity, a concern for justice and human welfare, a sense of human equality, and a love of human freedom, and a practice of brotherhood which are necessary to the life of our national institutions.[1]

When the meeting was over, I thanked him for what he had said, and added: "You sounded like a preacher tonight." To my surprise, he replied: "I thought about becoming one when I was young but I decided I wasn't good enough." I thought of this later when I discovered how many times he had read the Bible, and that he played the piano occasionally for the young peoples' meeting in his home church.

In a book which Mr. Truman wrote several years after he retired to Independence, entitled *Mr. Citizen,* there is a chapter with the heading "Reflections of a Grandfather." The following lines are in that chapter:

Most of my own ideas on how the world runs I obtained very early in life from the Bible, the King James version of the Old and New Testaments. The Bible is, among other things, one of the greatest

1. William Hillman, *Mr. President* (New York: Farrar, Strauss and Young, 1952) pp. 68, 69.

documents of history. Every trouble that humanity is heir to is set out in the Bible. And the remedy is there too, if you know where to find it. I read the Bible at least a dozen times, and maybe more, before I was fifteen years old. The Bible must be read over and over again to get the full meaning out of it. . . . And the moral code that is in the Old and New Testaments is needed by all mankind. If civilization is to continue, the majority of the people of the world must have a moral code by which to live, and by which to act. The moral code set forth in the Bible is unequaled. Of course, these youngsters in whom I am so vitally interested will be brought up on a moral code, I hope, based on the great code of the Old and New Testaments.

In another chapter of the same book, entitled, "My Views on Religion," Mr. Truman wrote: "I have been a voluntary member of the Baptist Church since I was eighteen years old. . . . My mother and father were Baptists, so was my Grandfather Truman and my Grandmother Young. Grandma Truman . . . was also a Baptist."

Recently, realizing that I would be passing through Missouri on my way to a convention, so I wrote to a friend in Kansas City and asked him if he could get the pastors who had been associated with the churches Mr. Truman attended to be my guests for lunch on the day I would be in Independence. He graciously complied with my request and I had the privilege of spending several hours with four of these pastors. I learned from them that the former president had made a substantial gift to the building fund of the Baptist Church in Grandview in 1953, and that he had appeared on the program on the day of dedication. While my conversation with the pastors did not include many specifics, the general impression I received seemed to support the conviction I had held for a long time, viz., that Mr. Truman's religious convictions were very genuine and sincere, but that he had not been in his adult life what we usually think of when we speak of a "churchman." From time to time as I would talk to him, I really got the impression that something in his boyhood experience had "set his teeth on edge" regarding the church. This impression gained support as I read other passages in the chapter on his religious views referred to above. For instance, he wrote:

> My Grandfather Young belonged to no church, but he supported many of them—Baptist, Methodist, Campbellite and Presbyterian. . . . Grandfather Young told me when I was six that all of them wanted to arrive at the same place but they had to fight about it to see who had the inside track with the Almighty. . . . My Grandfather Truman felt the same way. . . . All my family disliked a hypocrite. My Grandfather Young once told me, "When a man spends Saturday night and Sunday doing too much howling and praying, you had better go home and lock your smoke house."

Mr. Truman, later in the same chapter, spoke of his family as being "individualistic" and "independent" in arriving at personal views.

My experience with reporters during the years that the president was attending our church was generally very pleasant. However, occasionally I would be embarrassed by what they would write after interviewing me. On one occasion, in response to a reporter's question concerning the way in which our church arranged for the president's visits, I mentioned that according to a long established custom which other presidents had followed, and which was requested by the Secret Service, I would ask the congregation to be seated following the benediction, and would then go to the president's pew and walk with him to the street. When the article appeared in a news magazine, the definite impression given was that I had devised this procedure "in order to get the president's ear."

On another occasion, I was in New York City to attend a meeting of religious leaders in connection with the president's nomination of an ambassador to the Vatican (which I shall discuss in the next chapter), and a reporter for one of the New York papers asked me if I had discussed the nomination with the president that week. When I replied that I had not, she then asked if I expected to talk to him about it the *next* week, and I replied that I had made no plans to do so. I was to leave New York on a sleeper at midnight, and on my way to the station I picked up the first edition of the next day's paper. To my amazement I read that I had said: "I haven't seen the president this week, nor do I expect to see him next week." While the essential facts in the story were correct, the wording to me sounded flip and impudent. I checked my overnight bag in a locker at the station and went over to the editorial offices of the paper. As soon as I was able to locate a member of the night staff, I showed him the article and described my reaction to it. He seemed to agree that I had cause for complaint, and revised the article for the other editions. However, I never discovered which edition Mr. Truman saw.

There were also some humorous aspects to being pastor of the church which the president attended. When Mr. Truman was faced with the necessity of appointing a chief justice of the Supreme Court, two well-meaning individuals approached me with offers to assist him in meeting this grave responsibility. One man spent nearly four hours telling me his life's story, and why he felt competent to be helpful to the president, and then declared that God had revealed to him a method by which any man could discover His will; and had given him permission to pass this information on to me so that I could get it to the president and thereby make it possible for him to make the right choice for such a high office. The method was this: let your Bible fall open wherever it will; notice the last word on the top line of the right-hand page; if the word has an even number of letters, the answer is yes; if an odd number of letters, the answer is no. I looked at the man in amazement and wondered if he could be serious. Everything he had said up to that point was perfectly rational and believable. I soon discovered that he was entirely serious. However, I never revealed to the president this strange way of reaching decisions!

One morning, I found in my mail a letter from a lady whose letterhead indicated that she was the head of some new religious sect. She, too, was concerned over the Supreme Court appointment, and declared that God had revealed to her the name of the man the president should choose. She wanted me to arrange an appointment for her with the president so that she could pass on this information. In a letter of response to her, I indicated that my acquaintance with Mr. Truman led me to believe that he would be very responsive to divine guidance, and therefore I felt if God had a message for the president that He would convey it directly and not through another person. In a day or two, I received another letter from this lady indicating her displeasure with my reaction to her offer of help, and she said: "I was talking with God this morning, and He said to me, 'Martha, you tell Dr. Pruden that he should take more seriously your offer of assistance to the president." When I went home to dinner that night, I related this incident to my wife, and said to her that the part of the letter which really upset me was the inference that this lady was on a first-name relationship with the Lord while He referred to me as "Dr. Pruden"!

When the summer of 1948 arrived and the newspapers reported the preparations being made in Philadelphia for the Democratic National Convention, I became increasingly anxious to attend, not only because of my special interest in the probability of Mr. Truman's nomination for another term, but also because of my life-long fascination with political events. I therefore wrote a note to the president asking if he could arrange for me to have tickets to the

Convention Hall. My final decision to attend the Convention, if I could secure tickets, was made so late in the summer that I felt sure that only the president would be able to get any for me. Within a few days, I received the tickets and soon thereafter was on my way to the Convention. My seat was in the balcony and not far from the platform, so I had a perfect view of all the proceedings. Considerable opposition to Mr. Truman's nomination had arisen in some of the southern delegations because he had supported certain pieces of civil rights legislation, but once the choice was made and the president began his acceptance speech, you could almost feel the change in mood among the delegates. His address was repeatedly interrupted by hearty applause, and at its conclusion there was a standing ovation. I rode back to my hotel on one of the Convention buses and heard several expressions of surprise and delight with the way the president handled himself that night. Many of them had seen him face to face for the first time, and their appraisal of the man and his chances for reelection were considerably revised. While I was there, I wrote to the president, expressing my appreciation for the tickets and indicating how much I enjoyed the occasion. In his reply to me, he wrote: "I appreciated very highly your note from the Bellevue-Stratford on Thursday morning. Sorry I didn't get to see you in Philadelphia. It was quite a show and I think everything eventually came out all right." The letter was typed, and signed by the president, and at the bottom of the page he wrote by hand: "Hope you have a pleasant vacation."

As the campaign progressed that fall, Mr. Truman's chances for election seemed very slim to many. The polls showed him trailing Governor Dewey by a sizable margin, and the third-party efforts of former Vice President Henry Wallace were not helping any either. In some parts of the South, the president was still unpopular because of his civil rights sympathies; and in other areas of the country there were those who had not liked Mr. Roosevelt and were equally unimpressed with his successor. In certain areas, it was actually considered ill-advised to express favorable comments regarding Mr. Truman. Someone told the story of two men who met in a hotel lobby. One of them asked the other what he thought of the president, and his response was, "Come over here behind this column and I'll tell you." Once they were safely out of distance of the other occupants of the lobby, the man replied to the question by saying, "To tell the truth, I really like him!" My mother, who was so impressed by the president when she visited him in his office at the White House, said that as far as she was able to tell, she would be the only person in her small town in southern Virginia to vote for Mr. Truman, but when the ballots were counted, he had carried the town.

Mr. Truman spent election night in Kansas City, but returned to Washington in triumph a day or two later. I went to Union Station and joined hundreds of others in welcoming him back to the capital city. He remained, with Vice President Barkley and a few others, in his special car for a while before coming out to face the crowd. His cabinet members and close associates entered the car to greet him. I waited until most of these had passed through the car, and as I approached it, the president's appointments secretary recognized me and invited me in. When the president saw me, his face lighted up and he exclaimed, "There's my preacher!" After I shook his hand and offered my congratulations, he introduced me to Mr. Barkley. As the two rode in an open car from the station to the White House, thousands lined the streets to cheer as they went by. I was asked to serve on the inaugural committee and to give the invocation at the inaugural ceremonies.

There was heavy rain on the day before the inaugural and the day after, but Inaugural Day itself was a cold, crisp, beautiful day. My inaugural prayer was as follows:

> God of the nations, in whom we live and move and have our being, and from whom cometh every good and perfect gift, we pause at the beginning of this day's historic proceedings to invoke Thy blessings

upon this beloved country of ours, and upon all who serve her highest interests.

Grant to Thy servants, the President and Vice President of the United States, all needed wisdom, health and strength as they dedicate themselves today to the high offices to which they have been called. May they continue to lead us as they are led by Thee, in ways that make for domestic tranquility and international accord.

Bestow upon us, our Father, the happiness which is reserved for that nation whose God is the Lord. Through Jesus Christ, our Redeemer, we pray. Amen.

Later in the ceremonies, prayers were offered by Rabbi Samuel Thurman of St. Louis, and Archbishop Patrick A. O'Boyle of the Roman Catholic Diocese of Washington. As the president took his oath of office, his hand rested on two Bibles—one opened to the Beatitudes at the beginning of the Sermon on the Mount, and the other to the Ten Commandments. The Bibles were the White House copies which he had used when he took the oath of office following the death of Mr. Roosevelt, and a replica of the Gutenberg Bible which had been given to the president by the people of Independence, Missouri, his hometown. Following the ceremonies, the three members of the clergy who had offered prayers were invited to the luncheon inside the Capitol which was given in honor of the president and vice president. Mr. Truman expressed his appreciation to each of us for the part we had had in the proceedings. When the president persented me again to Mr. Barkley, he jokingly referred to his vice president as "a poor excuse of a Methodist!" Both of them seemed to be enjoying the occasion to the fullest.

VI

BREAKFAST WITH THE PRESIDENT

On the first Sunday in January, 1950, President Truman came to our 9:30 A.M. service, walking the eight blocks from the White House and accompanied by a Secret Service man. At the conclusion of the service, as we were walking out of church, he said to me: "One of the Secret Service men told me that he saw you at the airport when I returned to Washington from Missouri last Wednesday. Why didn't you let me know you were there?" I replied: "I had taken some visiting relatives of mine out to the airport so that they could see you, but I had no thought of disturbing your busy schedule by attempting to speak to you." The president then said: "Well, the next time you're around when I happen to be present, I hope you'll speak to me."

On the strength of this invitation, and without any previous thought, I said: "Mr. President, there *is* something I would like to do some day"; and when he asked me what it was, I answered: "I would like to come down some morning and go walking with you." He responded, "By all means. Come any time. I'll be glad to have you."

I waited for about a month, and choosing a clear, crisp Saturday morning in February, I went down to Blair House where the president and his family were living during the reconstruction of the interior of the White House. Not knowing how early the president took his morning walk, I arrived at the front gate at eight o'clock. I gave my name to the guard in the "pill box" outside, and he telephoned inside to see if it would be all right to let me in. In just a moment he got his answer and told me to go in. As I walked up the steps, the front door was opened by the president who extended to me a warm welcome. He asked: "Have you had breakfast?" I said, "No, I didn't know when you might be starting out on your walk so I came without waiting for breakfast." "Well," he said, "come right in and eat with me, I'm alone this morning. Mrs. Truman, Margaret, and Helen Traubel [the opera singer and Margaret's voice teacher] are sleeping late this morning since they came in rather late last night from a concert." We went into the dining room and had a typical American breakfast—grapefruit, bacon and eggs, toast, coffee, and jam. The president talked of numerous things and made his guest feel right at home.

Within a few moments, the president referred to a newspaper article of recent date announcing the return to this country of Mr. Myron C. Taylor from his post as personal representative of the president to the Vatican in Rome. While I do not recall whether the article definitely stated that this would conclude Mr. Taylor's mission, I do recall having the impression that such was the case. Mr. Taylor had been originally appointed to this post by President Franklin D. Roosevelt in 1940, and it created some criticism among Protestant church leaders at the time because they felt that the president had used this method of establishing some kind of semi-official relationship to the Vatican as a means of avoiding a controversial showdown with Congress which would surely have occurred had he sent to Congress a nomination for an ambassador to the Vatican. Mr. Truman inherited this arrangement from his predecessor, and permitted it to continue. Since some of my Baptist colleagues continued to criticize the president for allowing the arrangement to continue, I mentioned to him on one occasion that I did not wish to be associated with this criticism since it was not an official relationship transacted by our government but simply a personal emissary of the president. In 1947, the correspondence between Mr. Roosevelt and Pope Pius XII was published in a small, beautifully bound volume. Color photographs of Mr. Roosevelt and the pope were just inside the front covers of the book, and there was a full-page, color photograph of Mr. Truman opposite the preface which he had been asked to write. One morning in June, 1947, a courier from the White House came to my study and gave me a package. It contained this volume and a letter from the president in which he expressed appreciation for what he felt to be an understanding and tolerant attitude on my part. He had written a note under the color photograph of himself, and had signed it. Mr. Taylor's signature was on the first inside page.

Mr. Truman had said on several occasions that in the interest of world peace he was seeking to bring together both the spiritual and moral forces of the world, and I know that Mr. Taylor visited a number of religious leaders in various parts of the world in pursuit of the president's objective. I gathered from things I heard from time to time from persons connected with the National and World Councils of Churches that these overtures had not been too successful and that probably Mr. Taylor was not the best choice for such an assignment. There was, therefore, a sigh of relief on the part of many when news of this conclusion of Mr. Taylor's assignment was announced in the press. I have given this rather lengthy background material in order that it may be understood how shocked I was at the turn which the president's remarks took as our conversation continued. Evidently Mr. Truman felt that my refusal to join those who were critical of his use of Mr. Taylor's services indicated that I would be sympathetic to even closer ties to the Vatican.

In any case, as we sat at breakfast in Blair House that February morning, the president rather casually said: "I am considering the possibility of sending an ambassador to the Vatican in the near future." This information came to me like a bolt out of the blue, and I was so stunned that I did not know how to reply. There seemed to me a vast difference between a personal representative to the Vatican and a full-fledged diplomatic appointment which would have to be confirmed by the Senate, and which would thereby become an official action of the United States government.

Without waiting for a comment from me, Mr. Truman turned to other matters and soon indicated that the time had come for the walk. We put on our coats and hats, and, accompanied by several Secret Service men (some close by and others at a distance), we started on a twenty-minute walk which took us to the grounds around the Washington Monument. The president touched upon several items of interest to me having to do with his early political career, Margaret's singing career, and some of the opposition he was facing in the Congress. All the while, I was trying to think of what I should say to him regarding the possibility of an ambassador to the Vatican. I felt that it would be a serious mistake, and yet I did not wish to say anything that would make him sorry that he had told me, or that would make him reluctant to tell me anything else in the future. Since the right words never came to me, I concluded that I would give myself a little time to think the matter through before presenting any objections. Our walk ended at the door to the Executive Offices and, after expressing my appreciation of Mr. Truman's hospitality, I left for home and for a very miserable weekend. I knew I could not divulge to anyone else what the president had told me at his breakfast table until he had made some public announcement of it, and yet I knew that something had to be done to let the president know what I felt sure would be the reaction of most Americans to such an appointment.

By Monday morning I knew I had to see the president again, and therefore called his appointments secretary,

Matthew T. Connelly, to see when a visit would be possible. He informed me that the president was solidly booked for appointments until Friday afternoon. I told him that I really should see him before that time but would naturally wait until Friday since that was the only time available. That night, my wife was preparing dinner when the telephone rang, and when she picked up the receiver and answered, the person on the other end of the line said: "Mrs. Pruden, this is Harry Truman. Is your husband there?" When my wife recovered from the shock, she called me, and the president explained that he had learned that I was anxious to see him as soon as possible, and that since his appointment schedule was such that he could not see me until Friday, he was wondering if there were something he could do over the telephone. (This seemed so typical of Mr. Truman, for, as indicated in an earlier chapter, he always impressed me as being extremely thoughtful and considerate of others. This telephone call was one that he really did not have to make.) I replied that I wanted to talk with him further about the Vatican appointment to which he had referred at breakfast the previous Saturday morning. He responded by saying that consideration of the matter would cover a considerable period of time, and that, therefore, no immediate decision was anticipated. I thanked him for calling and told him that I would look forward to seeing him Friday.

Between Monday and Friday, I had ample time in which to think through and put down in writing what my own reaction to the Vatican proposal was, and what I felt sure the reaction of many Americans would be. Since appointments with the president are usually held to a fifteen-minute period, I did not undertake to read the five-page letter I carried with me. I simply spent the time on Friday discussing the matter generally and then asking for the privilege of leaving the letter with him. He accepted it very cordially. The following is an abbreviated version of the letter:

February 3, 1950

Honorable Harry S. Truman
The White House
Washington, D.C.

Dear Mr. President:

For fear we would not have sufficient time today to go into the Vatican question very thoroughly, I am taking the liberty of putting into writing, as briefly and as frankly as I can, my own reaction to the matter.

As I said to you last Saturday, I have always defended Mr. Taylor's presence at the Vatican on the grounds that he was there during an emergency in our nation's history, and that I felt sure the mission would be terminated at an early date. I have also explained to audiences in which the question has been raised that, while I felt inclined to defend Mr. Taylor's present mission, I would be unalterably opposed to any permanent mission at the Vatican, and certainly strongly opposed to any thought of reopening the formal diplomatic post which our government maintained at the Vatican many years ago. I also told people who asked me, that while I had never discussed the matter with you, and certainly I had no information as to how you felt, my own impression was that you probably felt the same way about the situation.

I would now like to list the reasons which compel me to regard such a move as a serious mistake:

(I) In the first place, it seems unnecessary in view of the fact that the Pope is certainly resourceful enough to devise some means by which any information or communication intended for our government could be supplied to our regular diplomatic ambassador to Italy. While this might be an irregular diplomatic procedure, nevertheless it would serve the purpose desired and at least prevent the explosion at home which is sure to occur if any suggestion is made that a formal diplomatic post be resumed.

(II) In the second place, I feel that while both a personal representative at the Vatican and a formal ambassador would both be opposed by the majority of the American people, nevertheless the presence of a personal representative in Rome would certainly be interpreted as the lesser of two evils. I am therefore wondering what a formal diplomatic post could achieve which has not been achieved by the personal representative.

(III) Since we trust that the present world emergency is a temporary thing, it would seem most unfortunate to establish a permanent post at the Vatican which would not only embarrass millions of Americans now, but which would continue to be an embarrassment in the future. Once having entered into such a relationship at the Vatican, it would be embarrassing to the Vatican itself to have the arrangement discontinued later.

(IV) Since our country is historically committed to a policy of the separation of church and state, it would seem to me practically impossible to justify a diplomatic relationship with a church-state union such as the Vatican now presents. I believe that worthy principles must be observed even in our diligent seeking to establish worthy objectives, and I cannot see how in the long run the principle of peace can be firmly established by disregarding a principle which has become so much a part of the fabric of our American way of life.

(V) Ever since Mr. Taylor resigned, the general public has been under the impression that the mission to the Vatican is at an end. Certainly the dispatch from Rome that his assistant was closing the office and returning to America for consultation gave the definite impression that the mission was to be permanently terminated. I have heard not the slightest hint either in the papers or in my personal conversations with scores of people that a formal diplomatic post might be reestablished. Such a proposal would fall like a bombshell among the American people.

I think it should be pointed out here that the leading figures among those who feel very strongly about this matter, and who have not only opposed Mr. Taylor's presence at the Vatican, but who would oppose even more vigorously any thought of a permanent post, are the most respected and intelligent minds among American Protestants today. I am aware that there are rabble-rousing individuals who hurt the cause they are trying to help, but the great concerted influence of the Protestant churches today is being expressed by men of outstanding intellectual ability who are recognized throughout the country for their liberalism and desire for Christian brotherhood with Catholics and all other followers of Christ—college presidents, seminary executives, magazine editors, outstanding laymen in places of prominence both in the business and professional life of the country. In fact, I don't know of a single recognized Protestant leader in America today who has been in favor of Mr. Taylor's presence at the Vatican in the past or who would not oppose strenuously the continuation of any sort of mission at the Vatican in the future.

(VI) There are millions of us who feel no prejudice or ill will toward the Catholic Church, and who would oppose just as vigorously any move within our own denomination to ignore our historical

American ideals. I think you know how sincerely I believe in the spirit of Christian unity and how happy it would make me to work in closer cooperation with Catholic Christians, but there are times when my conscience demands that I voice an honest conviction or oppose a move which I feel to be detrimental to the best interests of America.

In closing, Mr. President, may I say two things:

(1) I think you know me well enough to know that I am no anti-Catholic. I feel uncomfortable in the presence of men who reveal a prejudiced and bigoted attitude toward their fellow Christians of the Catholic faith.

(2) I have been, and shall remain, loyal to you whatever you may do in this matter, even though I would have to oppose, with whatever influence I may have, the establishment of a permanent post at the Vatican. If I ever voice any sentiments in public on the matter, I shall always make it plain that I am not opposing you personally, and that nothing I say on this particular matter must ever be interpreted as any lessening of the high regard and deep personal attachment which I feel for you. I am comforted in the thought that this will also be your attitude toward me.

With my fondest good wishes, I am

Most respectfully and sincerely,

(s) Edward H. Pruden

If any of the above seems exaggerated, it should be remembered that the letter was written twenty-five years ago. Today, both Protestants and Catholics are working diligently to create greater Christian cooperation and understanding. This does not mean that there would be today any more support for the appointment of an ambassador to the Vatican, but it *does* mean that Protestants and Catholics are now doing more things together, with the result that this increased knowledge of one another has made it possible for them to disagree on significant matters without suspecting that such differences are due to prejudice.

A few days after I left my statement with the president, I received a letter from him stating that he had read the material I had left with him and was sending it to the Secretary of State for his study. Then he expressed appreciation for my expression of personal loyalty and friendship which he said was genuinely reciprocated.

And a week later I received a letter from the Secretary of State, Mr. Dean Acheson, in which he expressed appreciation for my analysis of the proposed appointment and assured me that the objections I had raised were being carefully considered by his office. Several months went by before I heard anything more regarding the matter.

Some time in the late summer of 1950, there appeared a news story in the Washington papers saying that the president had under consideration the appointment of an ambassador to the Vatican. On August 10, there was an editorial in the *Washington Post* entitled, "Mission to the Vatican." The writer of the editorial not only gave his endorsement to the proposal but suggested that nothing but prejudice would interfere with congressional approval. I immediately addressed a letter to the editor of the *Post* in which I said:

> I have long been an admirer of the *Washington Post's* fair and reasonable editorial policy, and am therefore all the more surprised to see the contents of your editorial of August 10, "Mission to the Vatican." The whole trend of the editorial is to the effect that your own reasons for approving such a mission are entirely valid and that all views to the contrary are prompted by prejudice. This trend reaches its peak in the closing paragraph in these words: "It is possible,

perhaps even probable, that prejudice may even at this stage of affairs be strong enough to block senatorial confirmation of Mr. Truman's plan to nominate a regular diplomatic representative. But this is the sort of prejudice that the country can now ill afford." There are many of us who do not accept your reasoning at all, and yet feel that our reasons for opposing such a mission are above prejudice . . . If your editorial is any indication of the line of argument which is to be used by those who approve the mission to the Vatican, the discussion is going to be bitter indeed; and if your early charge of prejudice is intended to discourage any from speaking who may have honest and valid reasons for doing so, I can assure you that such an effort will fail . . . Many of us who will feel bound by conscience to oppose this mission admire the president a great deal, and therefore sincerely trust that nothing we say on this subject will be interpreted as any lack of respect or admiration for him. Certainly we can disagree without becoming disagreeable.

That fall a number of religious leaders got together to discuss what might be done to dissuade the president from making such an appointment. One such group requested Bishop G. Bromley Oxnam, of the United Methodist Church, and me to visit the president and convey to him our concern. Bishop Oxnam, whose area of ecclesiastical responsibility was the city of Washington, was not only a highly respected leader in the efforts of the churches to apply the Gospel to the social areas of life, but an eloquent exponent of religious liberty and the separation of church and state. I had gotten to know him in the ministers' club to which we both belonged, and admired him tremendously for his intellectual ability and his moral courage. Our request for an appointment with the president was granted. The president received us cordially and listened intently as we presented our case. We tried to convince Mr.

Truman that our opposition to his proposal of an ambassador to the Vatican was not opposition to the Catholic Church. We indicated that we would be equally opposed to the establishment of a diplomatic post at the headquarters of our own denominations, or at the headquarters of the World Council of Churches in Geneva, Switzerland. The president related to us several incidents in which he had demonstrated his own concern for religious freedom, citing his delay in recognizing Franco's government in Spain until he had some assurances that Protestant groups there would no longer be harrassed in their work. While the president was cordial and attentive to the Bishop and me, he gave no indication that he was disposed to alter his plans.

VII

RESPONSE TO THE
VATICAN APPOINTMENT

Almost a year went by before anything further was heard regarding the proposed diplomatic post. On Saturday, October 20, 1951, I was in my study at the church when my associate, R. Edward Dowdy, entered the room and laid on my desk a news release he had just received over the telephone. It had just been announced by the White House that the president had appointed General Mark Clark to be ambassador to the Vatican. A reporter for one of the news services had called me for a statement as to my reaction to the announcement. Mr. Dowdy had answered the telephone on the extension in his study, and since he knew that I would not want to make a statement "off the cuff," he had taken the message and told the reporter that I would call him back.

Both of us were shocked. Since nearly a year had elapsed since anything further had been said about the Vatican appointment, we had naturally assumed that the matter had been dropped. Mr. Truman had not mentioned the matter to me again, though I had seen him on a number of occasions both at the church and elsewhere. The news came at a rather inopportune time for me since I was rushing through some necessary work prior to taking my family to a football game at the University of Maryland. I decided to issue only a brief statement at the moment and prepare a longer one that night which I would read to my congregation the next morning, and which, of course, would be available to the press at that time. The brief statement was as follows:

I am very sorry that an ambassador has been appointed to the Vatican. I would equally oppose a like appointment to the world Baptist headquarters or the headquarters of any other religious body. It is my conviction that this is entirely contrary to our historic American position regarding the separation of Church and State. The President and I are both Baptists, and Baptists not only have a perfect right to differ among themselves, but are perfectly capable of doing this without any decline of personal relationships or mutual esteem.

The next day I read the following longer statement to my congregation at both morning services:

It was with deep regret that I learned yesterday that an ambassador had been nominated to represent our country at the Vatican. I believe such action to be in direct opposition to one of the most cherished American principles, viz., the separation of Church and State. Perhaps our most unique contribution to the world has been the ideal of religious liberty, and this ideal has found eloquent expression in America largely because we have kept Church and State separate. Any action which seems to abrogate this principle in our relationships with other nations is bound to have a serious effect upon the operation of this principle in the homeland.

Since a number of efforts have been made to mobilize and unify the moral forces of the world in a time of crisis, it seems particularly unfortunate that the divisive subject of Vatican representation should now be injected into our national and international scene.

In view of the fact that many in my congregation are wondering what I did to discourage the nomination of an ambassador to the Vatican, I want to say very frankly that I did all that was possible for anyone to do. Not only in an individual capacity, but in cooperation with other Protestant officials, I did my utmost to point out the great dangers which seemed to me to lie in such an arrangement.

Between now and the reconvening of Congress in January, every citizen who shares these views must use all honorable means to persuade the members of the Senate to refuse confirmation of this nomination. While those who have reached the conclusion that representation at the Vatican is wise are undoubtedly of the opinion that this is in the best interest of our country, many of us cannot honestly share this conclusion. We are therefore bound by conscience to voice our protest.

This is a matter of principle, not of personalities. I am sure that those who are responsible for this nomination would have us believe that their refusal to be influenced by substantial Protestant opinion is not to be interpreted as a personal affront to those who advised against it. I am therefore equally sure that these individuals will not feel that our opposition to the nomination is in any way directed against *them* personally. However much we may disagree with any within our own denomination, or with those of other religious bodies, on this vital matter, our words and actions must always reflect the most charitable and considerate spirit.

That same day, I mailed to the president a copy of my statement so that he would receive it directly from me and not from the press, and in order that he would have the full text in case only excerpts from it were printed. In the covering letter to the statement, I reiterated my previous word to him that my opposition was based on conscience and principle and not directed against him personally, nor against "my fellow Christians of the Catholic Church." I concluded with this paragraph:

> I hope you will not permit this difference of opinion to alter in any way your relationship to our church. It seems to me that you and I now have an ideal opportunity to demonstrate the true Baptist spirit, viz., to agree to differ but to unite to serve. Please be assured of a warm welcome here at the church whenever you desire to come.

In a letter to me later, Mr. Truman assured me that there was absolutely no feeling on his part with regard to my frank expression on the Vatican issue.

On October 21, 1951, the Sunday following the Saturday on which the White House announced the president's decision, *The New York Times* had a news story regarding reaction to the Vatican appointment. It quoted from the brief statement I had given the press in Washington on the day of the announcement, and quoted also several other Protestant clergymen. Some of these quotations were as follows:

> Dr. G. Bromley Oxnam, Methodist Bishop . . . and a president of the World Council of Churches: "I regret and I believe the President will regret this unwise, unnecessary and un-American decision."

> Presiding Bishop Henry Knox Sherrill of the Protestant Episcopal church, and president of the National Council of Churches: "I hope and believe that this unwise proposal will be opposed by the great majority of fair-minded Americans of every religious conviction, and will either be withdrawn or defeated in the Senate. . . . The overwhelming majority of the churches in the National Council of Churches of

Christ in America have already expressed their opposition to this proposal."

Dr. Franklin Clark Fry, president of the United Lutheran Church in America: "Along with millions of other American Lutherans I regard the appointment of an American ambassador to the Vatican as a breach of the American principle of separation of church and state. . . . It is ridiculous to pretend that this diplomatic recognition is being accorded to a tiny secular state. All the world knows that the Ambassador is to be sent to the Pope as a powerful religious leader. I hope that the United States will rebuff this assault on historic American principle."

Dr. Harold Bosley [then pastor of the First Methodist Church in Evanston, Illinois] was quoted as feeling that the appointment was made to "strengthen the Democratic machine, particularly in the big cities."

The following day, Monday, October 22, 1951, *The New York Times* carried my picture on its front page and a two-column headline which read: "Truman Pastor Tried to Bar Naming of Envoy to Vatican." The article which followed contained quotations from the longer statement which I had read to my congregation on the previous day, and brief reactions from some who approved the action and from others who opposed it. Among those who approved were Archbishop Richard J. Cushing of Boston, later a cardinal of the Catholic Church, who was quoted as saying: "Everyone who is generally interested in the attainment of world peace will hail this action with enthusiasm." Representative Franklin D. Roosevelt, Jr., Democratic representative from New York's Twentieth District, who had just returned from Europe, declared that he was "very pleased because I have long urged the Administration to renew diplomatic relations with the

Vatican; as a matter of fact, I recommended this move about a week ago in a short-wave broadcast from Rome to the United States." Mr. Roosevelt then added that in an audience with Pope Pius XII, he had been assured that the Vatican would "welcome a renewal of diplomatic relations with the United States."

Among those who were being quoted as being in opposition were the following:

Dr. Eugene Carson Blake, stated clerk of the General Assembly of the Presbyterian Church in the United States (and later General Secretary of the World Council of Churches): "Such diplomatic recognition of one church by our government is deliberately to flout the expressed wishes and deeply held convictions of most Protestants."

Prof. Henry P. Van Deusen, President of Union Theological Seminary in New York made public a telegram to Mr. Truman in which he said he wished to "add my personal voice to the storm of protests from loyal Americans who are justly outraged, both by your nomination of an American Ambassador to the Vatican and by the timing of its announcement."

Dr. Robert J. McCracken, pastor of the Riverside Church, New York City, said that the president's action "flouts Protestant conviction on a matter of basic principle and leaves Protestants with no choice save that of uncompromising opposition and rejection."

Dr. Ralph W. Sockman, pastor of Christ Church, Methodist, said: "The appointment of an Ambassador to the Holy See is a dangerous threat to the American principle of the separation of church and state . . . and . . . is a betrayal of the principle for which many came to our shores."

Within the next few days, I began receiving invitations to speak in various places on the implications of the appointment. My first impulse was to decline all of them since I felt that I had made my point and, frankly, I disliked the idea of becoming involved further in a debate which would surely give the impression to many that opponents to the appointment were anti-Catholic and narrow-minded. I did accept an invitation to speak at a city-wide Reformation Day service in Trenton, New Jersey, because I felt that this would give me an opportunity to clarify my position and perhaps help to shape the type of opposition that would be offered. Some portions of that address are as follows:

We have not the slightest desire to engage in religious controversy, and if anything we say seems to involve such a controversy, it will be due entirely to the fact that a delicate and involved situation has been thrust upon us. There are times when our consciences require of us that we speak, even though we know in advance that we will be misunderstood and misinterpreted. This is a burden which we must be prepared to carry, knowing that others have carried it before us in the age-long struggle of the human spirit to keep itself free. . . . Nearly two years ago when the Pope of the Roman Church extended to all Christians an invitation to unite with the Church of Rome in order that a common front might be created against communistm, I undertook to respond to that invitation in the most considerate and charitable fashion. In fact, I used as a sub-title these words: "A sincere attempt to give a brotherly answer to an invitation sincerely extended." In that message I declared that I was presenting my response "in the most sympathetic and brotherly spirit" and that "again and again in private conversation, and publicly from the pulpit," I had urged my congregation to maintain a friendly and brotherly attitude toward their fellow-Christians of the Roman communion. In spite of this cautious and considerate approach to the matter, my message was heralded in the press as being an attack upon the Catholic Church; and scores of letters came to me . . . denouncing me for being a bigot and a disturber of religious harmony. I have therefore come to the conclusion that if we wish to avoid this kind of misinterpretation, we must refrain from expressing ourselves at all. However, that would be a cowardly one for any disciple of Christ to make. We must speak frankly but kindly, and leave the outcome in the hands of God.

Later in the address, the objections to the appointment which I mentioned were those which I had listed in my letter to the president following our breakfast together in February, 1950.

I was also asked to appear on a nationwide television show entitled *Keep Posted,* a program sponsored by *The Saturday Evening Post,* with Lawrence Spivak and Martha Roundtree as co-hosts. At first I declined, suggesting several other names of persons I felt should be enlisted for this particular program, but was finally persuaded to accept. The other guest on the program was a Catholic priest who taught at Brooklyn College. He spoke first on his approval of the appointment and I followed with my points of disapproval. A panel of citizens had been gathered by the program directors, chaired by a former ambassador to Poland, Arthur Bliss Lane. I had no idea how to prepare for the program because there was no way of knowing what questions would be asked. However, I was pleased with the questions that *were* asked since they proved to be the ones for which I felt that I had an answer. Most of them seemed to indicate that the questioner could see no difference in a diplomatic mission to the Vatican and our diplomatic ties with Great Britain where the reigning monarch is considered the head of the Church of England; or our one-time diplomatic mission to the Sheik of Baghdad, who was head of the religious establishment of his state. My answer, of course, was to the effect that both of the examples cited represented missions to states having extensive commercial dealings with the United States, and that the fact that the rulers of these states occupied positions of religious significance was purely incidental. On the other hand, Vatican State is a minute tract of land surrounded by the city of Rome with no commercial interests whatever apart from a barber shop and the souvenir stalls in and around St. Peter's Basilica. The only thing of significance at the Vatican is a religious institution. A few days later, I received a letter from Mr. Spivak, saying that the station had had an extraordinarily good reaction to the program.

In recent months, the Westminster Press has published the *Memoirs* of Dr. W.A. Visser 't Hooft, long-time general secretary of the World Council of Churches, whose office was in Geneva. In the volume, the author speaks of a "discreet inquiry" which was made by our government regarding the possibility of sending a United States ambassador to the World Council of Churches. In correspondence with Dr. Visser't Hooft since the publication of his book, I learned that while he is unable to pinpoint the exact time the "discreet inquiry" was made, he is of the opinion that it was made around the time the Vatican debate was going on here at home. One cannot help but wonder if this was a totally isolated incident or if it was thought that ties with the World Council might make the Vatican mission more palatable to Protestants.

In his book, Dr. Visser 't Hooft discusses the negotiations which took place between the World Council officials and the Vatican by which it was hoped that Roman Catholic observers might attend the First Assembly of the World Council to be held in Amsterdam in 1948. Then we come upon this paragraph:

In the meantime the situation had been further confused by the intervention of Mr. Myron Taylor, the American industrialist who had been sent to Rome, originally by President Roosevelt, as the personal representative of the President of the United States to the Pope. He came to see me and explained that at the request of President Truman he was visiting several religious leaders. He would see Pastor Boegner in Paris and the Archbishop of Canterbury in London. He expressed the conviction that all who believed in God and in freedom should be brought together to fight communism. We should therefore invite to the Assembly representatives of national governments engaged in this fight. It was clear that he wanted to come to Amsterdam himself. . . . He also expressed astonishment that we had not invited the leaders of Islam to participate in the meeting. I could only tell him that he had misunderstood completely what the World Council really was. Our sole purpose was to manifest the fundamental unity of the Christian churches. Mr. Taylor did not think that it was necessary to have Christ mentioned. I explained that we were trying to bring all Christian churches together including the Eastern European churches and those of the USSR. Mr. Taylor did not like the idea. I told him that we wanted to remain completely independent of governmental influences. So between his conception of the role of the church and ours there was such a wide gulf that it seemed impossible to make him understand what we were after.[1]

In describing World Council affairs three years after the incident referred to above, Dr. Visser 't Hooft wrote:

A further complicating factor at this time was the

1. W. A. Visser 't Hooft, *Memoirs* (Philadelphia: Westminster Press, 1973), p. 207.

activity of Myron Taylor, still acting on behalf of President Truman. After the failure of his approach to the World Council in 1948 which I have described already, the President and Mr. Taylor had worked out a new proposal. The president would invite the heads of the Christian churches to come to Washington and to work together on a joint statement concerning peace and concerning common resistance to communism. When Mr. Taylor submitted this proposal to two of the presidents of the World Council, Pastor Marc Boegner in Paris and the Archbishop of Canterbury in London, both turned it down. It was inconceivable that church leaders should come to Washington to work out a common statement under the auspices of the President of the United States. Pastor Boegner had had occasion in 1950 to tell President Truman personally that the churches were working for peace, but that they could not possibly participate at the request of a temporal power in a crusade the political and religious character of which would endanger their spiritual independence. But Mr. Taylor returned to the attack. The form which the proposal now took was that the Pope and the leaders of the World Council of Churches should produce a common statement along the lines of President Truman's ideas. In the summer of 1951 he met in London with the Archbishop of Canterbury, the Archbishop of York, the Bishop of Chichester and presiding Bishop Sherrill of the Protestant Episcopal Church in the United States. The difficulty on this as on earlier similar cases was that it was not clear what President Truman and Mr. Taylor had in mind.[2]

Dr. Visser 't Hooft then points out that in 1950 one of the

2. Ibid., p. 225-226.

constituent churches in the World Council had submitted to the Council a request that the Council should appeal to the churches outside its constituency "to agree that all churches together should coordinate their efforts and unite their prayers 'so that the peace of God may come upon the nations'."[3] After extended consideration of this proposal, the World Council's Executive Committee rejected it, based primarily upon a realistic appraisal of the chances such a proposal would have in certain quarters. Reporting its decision to the Central Committee of the Council in the summer of 1951, the Executive Committee declared: "For the World Council to seek to join with great churches outside its membership in a general peace appeal now is not a practicable policy and its pursuit would not help the general situation."[4] Then Dr. Visser 't Hooft adds:

> When Mr. Taylor saw this report he must have taken this sentence, which was originally simply an answer to a member church of the World Council, as a public repudiation of the plan on which President Truman and he were working. On September 28 President Truman reacted sharply. He said publicly that he had for some time tried to bring the leaders of the churches together, but that they had been unable "to say with one voice, that Christ is their Master and Redeemer and the source of their strength against the hosts of irreligion and danger to the world and that will be the cause of world catastrophe." Very soon afterwards the President announced that he would propose the appointment of an ambassador to the Vatican. . . .
> My role in this tangled episode was to disentangle the various developments. At the end of a long letter to Franklin Clark Fry in which I tried to analyze

3. Ibid., p. 26.
4. Ibid.

what had really happened I wrote: "The misunderstanding which has arisen between President Truman and the church leaders is not half as serious as the misunderstanding which would have arisen if we had given any encouragement to Mr. Taylor in his confused plans of mixing up Church and State." Fry expressed his agreement in much stronger phraseology than mine.

I believe that it was in this same period that I received a discreet inquiry whether we would be interested in having an ambassador from the USA accredited to the World Council in Geneva. I replied that I could only give a very provisional reaction, which was that I had no idea what to do with such an ambassador. Fortunately no more was heard about this. For was it not like asking the manager of a china shop, after he had a visit from a bull, whether he would like to have the bull as a permanent guest?[5]

I don't believe Mr. Truman ever understood why the World Council leaders did not respond favorably to his overtures. In a letter to me in August, 1952, he expressed again his desire to unite the moral forces of the world against the powers that sought to suppress human freedom, and suggested that jealousy between the various religious groups had made his task all the more difficult. He indicated, however, that he still had hope for peace in the world and would continue working for it.

While I sincerely believe Mr. Truman made the appointment to the Vatican for the very purpose he stated, viz., in order to have better access to information available at the Vatican's Foreign Office, I shall always be puzzled at the timing of the appointment, and the person he nominated for the office. The appointment was made in October just as the

5. Ibid., pp. 226, 227.

Congress was winding up its session for the year, which meant that the appointment would have to lie on the table until January when the next session of the Congress would convene. This meant that those who opposed the appointment would have three months in which to marshall their forces in opposition to it. The person the president selected for this office, as indicated earlier, was General Clark, and a special act of Congress would be required in order for an army officer to serve as an ambassador. Furthermore, it was necessary for the Foreign Affairs Committee of the Senate to consider and approve the nomination before it could go to the Senate for consideration. The chairman of the Foreign Affairs Committee at that time was Senator Tom Connally of Texas, and it was reported that the Senator did not have a high regard for General Clark because a number of Texas soldiers were lost in a World War II battle which General Clark is supposed to have directed, and the rumor was that Senator Connally did not believe that the general had used good judgment in planning the strategy for the battle.

In addition to the handicaps mentioned above, the tide of opposition continued to roll in. While I have no way of knowing what the president's thoughts were during these weeks, I am inclined to believe that he was surprised at the scope and intensity of the objections raised. A member of his Cabinet told me that the president said to him that he thought the whole thing would blow over in a few weeks. This, however, was not the case. An official of the State Department later confided to me that the avalanche of mail in opposition to the appointment which arrived at the Department exceeded anything in his memory. In any case, before the Senate had time to consider the appointment, General Clark requested that his name be withdrawn from consideration for the post, and that brought to a conclusion the whole matter.

During these weeks, the president did not come to church. Someone told me that one Sunday morning he attended a flower show, and as he was leaving the building, he was asked: "Mr. President, are you going to church from here?" The president is reported to have replied: "No. My preacher and I have had a fight." Someone else said that Mr. Truman told a visitor to his office one day that the preachers were stirring up lots of dust over the Vatican issue, and that his preacher was the worst of all!

It was around this time that an attempt to assassinate him was made and I do know that the Secret Service placed new and much more severe restrictions on his movements thereafter. The old church building in which we were worshipping at that time was not the safest place in the world for a public figure whose life might be in danger. The sanctuary, as stated earlier, was on the second floor of the structure, and could be reached only by negotiating a long flight of stairs. Mr. Truman's pew was on the main floor of the sanctuary between two balconies. It was, therefore, impossible to say whether his absence from our church for the remaining year of his administration was due entirely to his displeasure over my opposition to his appointment or whether it was due in part to the limited number of public appearances he made during that time. In any case, we had some correspondence during those months and his letters were as cordial and friendly as ever.

During the years of his retirement in Independence, I was in the area for conventions or committee meetings on several occasions, and I always paid a visit to his office. He could not possibly have been more hospitable or thoughtful. On one occasion when he was visiting in Washington, he walked over from his hotel to see our new church building and he seemed to be delighted with it. On another visit to Washington, I took my youngest son to see him in his room at the Mayflower Hotel. Our daughter, Patricia, and our older son, Dick, had met the president at the time he was attending our church. Edward, however, was born just a short time before the president retired to Independence. As we were going up on the elevator, my son, then nine years of age, said: "What can I talk about to the President of the United States?" I said: "Mr. Truman is quite a historian. Why don't you ask him some question about your latest history assignment in school?" So, he did, and after a warm greeting from Mr. Truman, the two of them sat on a sofa together and talked about the Battle of Trenton during the Revolutionary War. After a few moments, Mr. Truman said, "Edward, don't you let that picture of Washington crossing the Delaware fool you. You remember that there is a flag flying from the back of his boat. Well, we didn't even have a flag at that time!" I had carried my camera to the room, so I asked the president for permission to take a picture of the two of them before we left. As I am writing these words, I have before me on my desk a prized color picture of the president, smiling broadly, and holding Edward's right hand in both of his own. When Edward mailed it to him for his autograph, Mr. Truman complied with the request, and in reply asked for a copy of the picture for himself.

It was also during these retirement years that Mr. Truman learned that my wife and I were to be in Europe on a mission to the United States servicemen who were stationed there. To our surprise, and without any request from us, he sent to us a letter to American officials in Europe, written on his stationery, asking that courtesies be extended to us while we were there. The wording was as follows:

TO ALL AMBASSADORS,
CONSULS AND OTHER OFFICIALS
OF THE AMERICAN GOVERNMENT ABROAD:

This will introduce Dr. and Mrs. Edward Hughes Pruden, who are making a tour of Europe.

Dr. Pruden is the minister of the First Baptist Church in Washington, D.C., where I attended services when I was President.

Any courtesies that you can show Dr. and Mrs. Pruden will be highly appreciated by me.

/s/Harry S. Truman

On the last Sunday of Mr. Truman's administration, I concluded my sermon with these words:

> I cannot close this message without voicing a word of appreciation to him who has been our president for nearly eight years, and who has served our country with such faithfulness and devotion. I have not always agreed with his policies, but I have never doubted his sincerity, nor his desire to administer the affairs of our nation faithfully and well. None of us will ever know how heavy his burdens have been, nor how numerous have been the dark valleys through which he has had to pass. As we hail the new Chief, we would say "Thank you" to the leader who is now retiring to private life; and we commend them both to the mercies of God who alone can determine the destinies of nations. May His peace and grace be upon us all. Amen.

VIII

THE EISENHOWER PERIOD

There was a time during Mr. Truman's occupancy of the White House when it was rumored that the president, on one of his visits to Europe, had explored with General Dwight D. Eisenhower the possibility of the general's acceptance of the Democratic nomination for the presidency in 1952. However, even if the rumor were true, nothing occurred later to indicate that the general was interested. When, in the spring of '52, it was evident that Senator Robert A. Taft of Ohio was waging a strenuous campaign to capture the Republican nomination, other prominent members of that party urged the general to consent to being nominated at the convention to be held that summer. While Mr. Taft was tremendously popular with the conservative element in his party, he was not the type of person either personally or politically who was able to attract a large following among more liberal Republicans and Independents. It was said by some that almost any respected Democrat could be expected to win over Mr. Taft and that General Eisenhower would defeat the best candidate that the Democrats could possibly put forward.

All reports, however, indicated that the General showed little interest in such a political career. In fact, Mr. Truman, in his *Memoirs,* tells of a visit which the general made to the White House while he was chief of staff, during which visit the president asked him if he was considering running for the presidency. The general replied that he was not, and then informed Mr. Truman of a letter which he had written to a friend in which he expressed the opinion that it was not in the best interest of the country for a military man to become chief executive of the nation.[1] However, the Republicans who preferred the general over Mr. Taft did not give up. Later, while talking with Senator Frank Carlson of Kansas, one of the general's most enthusiastic supporters, I was impressed by his account of the extent to which the general's friends went in seeking to persuade him to let them place his name in nomination. It was generally recognized at that time that a popular military hero would stand an excellent chance of recapturing the White House for the Republicans after twenty years of Democratic occupancy. This reasoning proved to be valid.

From reports available to the public, it seemed that while General Eisenhower had been reared in a family connected with the religious sect known as River Brethren, he was not affiliated with any denomination at the time of his election. He had spent most of his life in military service, living in various places, and seldom being stationed anywhere long enough to become affiliated with a local church. Mrs. Eisenhower was a Presbyterian. Ten days following his inauguration, the general was baptized and became a member of the National Presbyterian Church. The Eisenhowers attended this church during his eight years as president.

Some time after he assumed the presidency, General Eisenhower invited the pastors of the Washington area to visit him at the White House. On this occasion, he spoke to us briefly, after which the president of our group Dr. Albert P. Shirkey, pastor of the Mount Vernon Place Methodist church, presented the president with a copy of the Revised Standard Version of the Bible on behalf of those present.

During his first year in office, the president attended the annual Prayer Breakfast at the Mayflower Hotel which was

1. Harry S. Truman, *Memoirs* (Garden City, N.Y.: Doubleday & Co., Inc.) Vol. II, p. 187.

sponsored by an interdenominational religious organization. Senator Carlson was the toastmaster for the occasion and, being a regular attendant at our church, he invited me to sit at the speakers' table and to offer the invocation. During the breakfast, I was able to speak with the president briefly and to present him with a printed copy of a sermon I had delivered on the Sunday before his inauguration, entitled, "The New President and the American People."

The sermon I presented to the president began with a brief presentation of the New Testament doctrine concerning constituted authority and the Christian's duty to recognize his citizenship obligations. This was followed by a warning lest an unfair standard be applied to an international military hero upon his assumption of the presidency, pointing out that a person moving suddenly from one type of service to another deserves sufficient time in which to adjust to an entirely new set of responsibilities. The following are paragraphs contained in the remainder of the sermon:

> The President of the United States deserves more sympathy and understanding than he usually gets. Criticizing the President is a favorite indoor sport among Americans. Not one of them has been immune and some of the best have been most severely denounced. When we pass the stately Lincoln Memorial in Washington today, and see the Great Emancipator enshrined in such splendor, it is hard to imagine how some of his contemporaries could have spoken of *him* in such uncomplimentary terms.

> The tendency to criticize the President may be one expression of our democracy. We want to make sure that no man thinks of himself more highly than he ought to think, or even gets the idea that he occupies a position so exalted that he can no longer be criticized. Criticism of a President may also be a hangover from our pioneering days when we broke away from the social patterns of the Mother Country in which titles were given to some and withheld from others.

However, before we exercise too freely our right to be critical of the President, let us remind ourselves of several things. For one thing, we are living in one of the gravest hours of history, and the President is carrying heavier burdens than any of us can ever imagine. The *Washington Post,* in an editorial recently, referred to the "impossible office of the President of the United States." President Truman, in his farewell address lask week, referred to some of the terrifying decisions he had been called upon to make during his years in office, and of the loneliness he frequently felt as he was confronted by these tremendous decisions.

And now, having said that, I want to make it plain that such respect and sympathy for the President does not mean that we must always approve what he does, or remain silent if he makes a proposal which our consciences cannot approve. We must be true to our convictions even as we want him to be true to his, and while there may be times when we must oppose what he has suggested, that oppostion should be courteously and respectfully presented, and without ever impugning the President's motives.

From all reports, President Eisenhower was regular in his church attendance, and always took his spiritual commitments seriously. He closed his inaugural address with a prayer which he had composed for the occasion, and when he retired to Gettysburg at the end of his term of office, he had his 'minister conduct a dedication service for the home which the Eisenhowers had established there. Late in his administration, the president traveled to Evanston, Illinois, to address the delegates to the General Assembly of the World Council of Churches.

When President Eisenhower appointed Governor Earl Warren of California as chief justice of the Supreme Court of the United States, the new chief justice came to Washington to assume his new duties while Mrs. Warren remained in

California for a few weeks to take care of the necessary details of moving to Washington. I had met the Warrens earlier when they had attended our church in connection with their visit to Washington in 1949 to attend the inauguration of President Truman. Two or three years later I had sat with the governor at the speakers' table in Oakland, California, when both of us spoke to the annual meeting of the Northern California Council of Churches. During the course of the evening, he questioned me regarding Mr. Truman's church attendance and the arrangements made by the church on the Sundays he was present in the congregation. I recalled at the time that Governor Warren had been the Republican vice presidential candidate on the same ticket with Mr. Dewey in the fall of 1948, and that it was the opinion of many that if the ticket had been reversed, the Republicans would have had a better chance of winning the election. I had also heard that Governor Warren would be a strong contender for the presidential nomination when the Republican Convention would meet in 1952. I therefore assumed that the governor's inquiries concerning the arrangements for a president's visit to church were not altogether academic. In any case, I was tremendously impressed with Governor Warren's earnestness, the depth and character of the man, and would have been pleased indeed to see him become our nation's chief executive.

After coming to Washington, Mr. Warren came regularly to our church, and later, during the construction of our new sanctuary, he worshipped with us in the Jewish Community Center. He and Mrs. Warren usually attended the anniversary dinners held by our church.

It was during the Eisenhower years that we finally realized the dream of our new sanctuary. For eighteen years we had been planning the structure, completing the scheme for the stained glass windows, and raising the necessary funds. Christmas Day in 1955 fell on Sunday, and it was on that day we held the first services in the sanctuary. There were two worship services that morning, as usual, and some of us, as we lifted our voices in thanksgiving, could not help but think of the words of the old hymn:

> None of the ransomed ever knew
> How deep were the waters crossed;
> Or how dark was the night when the Lord
>   passed through
> Ere He found His sheep that was lost;

for the congregation generally could never really know all the delays, reverses, disappointments, and other problems we had actually faced during the nearly two decades in which this House of God was becoming a reality. On Sunday night, a week later, we had as our guests four other downtown churches with which we had occasional joint musical services, and the preacher on that occasion was Dr. Joseph R. Sizoo, distinguished Presbyterian minister and, at that time, head of the Department of Religion at George Washington University. We felt adequately compensated for all the efforts expended when, in his introductory remarks, Dr. Sizoo said: "This sanctuary will make it easy for men to think of God, and difficult to forget Him." Much of the credit for this was due to the consecrated efforts of Harold Wagoner, the architect, and Henry Lee Willet, the designer of the windows, both devout churchmen.

We were anxious for the windows to reflect something of our basic convictions as well as some of the spiritual history to which we had fallen heir. The rose window above the communion table is the Resurrection Window, containing the ancient symbols of the life everlasting. The great window over the main entrance to the sanctuary is the Redemption Window, containing the symbols of God's provision for man's salvation, and likenesses of the personalities who proclaimed what God had done for mankind in Jesus Christ. Our New Testament heritage is portrayed in the major windows on either side of the sanctuary in sixty-four scenes from the life and ministry of Christ. Then, in two other series of smaller windows, our denominational heroes and other Christian worthies are portrayed. Our denominational heroes include William Carey, Adoniram Judson, John Bunyan, Alexander Maclaren, Luther Rice, B. H. Carroll, George W. Truett, Lottie Moon, Booker T. Washington, George Washington Carver, Walter Rauschenbusch, and Kenneth Scott Latourette. Some of the great Christians of history to whom all the Christian world is indebted are represented in the windows by Augustine, Luther, Calvin, Wesley, Grenfell, William Temple, Albert Schweitzer, Dwight L. Moody, and John R. Mott.

Some of the windows possess a special meaning to the church in that they were given by friends of other denominations. A prominent Methodist layman gave the Wesley window; Dr. William M. Elliott, Jr., my longtime friend, and pastor of the Highland Park Presbyterian Church in Dallas, along with certain friends in his church, gave the Calvin window: Dr. C. Leslie Glenn, rector of St. John's Episcopal Church in Washington, another friend of many years, gave the Phillips Brooks window in conjunction with certain members of his parish; and Dr. J. H. Jernagin, an outstanding black Baptist pastor in Washington, and also a close friend of mine, raised funds among the predominantly black churches for the Booker T. Washington and George Washington Carver windows.

During the years that the new sanctuary was being planned, we began collecting stones from churches around the world to be placed in the walls of our new church building. In time, we had stones from a church in Japan which was destroyed by one of the atom bombs; a stone from a mission church in Africa; one from a church in Argentina; and one each from Westminster Abbey and St. Paul's Cathedral in London. In the summer of 1955, while attending the Congress of the Baptist World Alliance, I visited St. Paul's Cathedral and found a stonemason repairing the white marble high altar which had been damaged during a bombing raid in World War II. He graciously gave me a fragment from this historic place. The small stone from Westminster Abbey I picked up on the lawn surrounding the historic church and which had fallen from an upper portion of the edifice. These fragments of stone and marble remind us that our church is not just a local congregation but a part of "the body of Christ" around the world.

IX

THE KENNEDY-JOHNSON DECADE

The first impressions of any significance I can recall regarding John F. Kennedy were those I received during the Democratic National Convention in Chicago in 1956. I took my family on a western trip that summer, and on our way home we charted an itinerary which would take us by Chicago at the time the Democrats were meeting there. We got a room in a motel on the outskirts of the city and watched the proceedings on television. Since Mr. Kennedy was then an active candidate for the vice presidency, the cameras frequently focused upon him and his brother, Robert, as they conferred or as either of them would answer questions from reporters. It had become so commonplace previously to be treated to the razzle-dazzle of political conventions and the accustomed campaign oratory that it was truly refreshing to see and hear two young men who spoke with such dignity, intelligence, and obvious sincerity, and to hear them discuss the issues with an unusual objectivity.

My first meeting with the future president took place on the Senate floor three or four years later. I had given the prayer at the opening of the session and, during a lull in the proceedings while a quorum roll call was being taken, I was invited to come down from the rostrum to the floor of the chamber by one of the senators who attended our church. He then called several of the senators over to a corner of the chamber and introduced me to them. Among them was Mr.

115

Kennedy. In the course of our conversation, I reminded him of the controversy over the Vatican appointment which had taken place seven or eight years previously, and stated that while he might not recall that I was somewhat involved in that unfortunate event, nevertheless I wanted to assure him that my concern had been primarily with the threat to our traditional practice of keeping Church and State separate and had not been directed against the Catholic Church. He indicated that he did remember the incident and had been aware of the reasons for my opposition. I got the definite impression that he too shared the conviction of most Americans that this historic principle should remain intact.

After Mr. Kennedy had received the Democratic nomination in the summer of 1960, and the campaign for the presidency progressed, there were numerous statements of concern from various groups and individuals, particularly from Protestant clergymen, as to the wisdom of electing a Roman Catholic to the highest office in the land. It was probably in response to such statements of concern that Mr. Kennedy agreed to address the Ministerial Union of Houston, Texas, and to answer questions at the conclusion of his address. This conference was televised nationally, or at least taped and televised later. In any case, I saw it more than once during the remainder of the campaign that fall and was greatly impressed by Mr. Kennedy's complete commitment to religious freedom and the separation of Church and State. I was also impressed by the answers he gave to the questions that were asked. I think I have never heard a finer delineation of our American heritage in this area of our common life. I jokingly accused one of our Baptist experts on this subject of having written the speech for Mr. Kennedy, and, while he denied the charge, I got the impression that he was ready to admit that he could not have expressed it better. In view of the candidate's forthrightness and his disarming expressions of personal convictions regarding basic issues, I felt that it was unfair and un-American to suggest that he should not be considered for the presidency because of his Catholic affiliations. As a consequence, on a Sunday morning late in October, I mentioned to my congregation during the announcement period, the campaign of opposition to Mr. Kennedy based on his religion, and stated that this campaign had reached the point at which all ministers could be suspected of sharing these views if they remained silent. I then declared that I did not wish to be associated with such views, and that while I did not want my statement to be considered a political endorsement of Mr. Kennedy, nevertheless I wanted to say emphatically that I thought it wrong to suggest that any American should be barred from any public office because of his religion.

On the night before Mr. Kennedy was inaugurated, one of the biggest snowstorms in Washington's history descended upon the city. Since the inauguration eve is always a time for parties in celebration of the historic event, thousands of Washingtonians drove to the downtown hotels to be a part of this celebration. When the parties were over and the guests prepared to return home, they discovered how heavy the snowfall had been. Those who were fortunate enough to have parked in indoor parking facilities soon discovered that many of the streets had not been cleared, and those that *were* cleared were so slick that travel was treacherous. Those who had parked on the streets found their cars almost out of sight. Since the hotels had been solidly booked for some time in anticipation of the inauguration, most of the marooned had to get what sleep they could in hotel lobbies.

During the night, the street crews cleared the inaugural line of march from the Capitol to the White House, and the sidewalks and bleachers where the public would view the parade, but the next morning, cold and clear, found most of us on streets still heavily covered with snow. We either walked, took a bus, or used a combination of the two in reaching the seats in the bleachers which we had reserved. My son, then ten years of age, and I started early and reached our seats in ample time to see the parade go by. Since the temperature was around freezing, there were numerous empty seats that had been paid for weeks before. By waving at the various units in the parade as they went by, and occasionally jumping up and down, we managed to keep our blood circulating. Our seats were across from the Presidential Box which was enclosed, and, I suppose, heated, so of added interest was the ability to watch the new president, his family, and close friends react to the proceedings. As the shadows lengthened, and the temperature began to drop perceptibly, there seemed to be no end to the bands and floats, so we decided that we had witnessed enough history for one day and returned home to thaw out.

A few months later, friends of the president arranged a gala birthday dinner for him at the National Guard Armory. The chaplain of the senate, Dr. Frederick Brown Harris, was asked to give the invocation, and I was invited to give the benediction. There must have been over a thousand people present. Mr. Truman traveled to Washington from Independence for the occasion, and since those who were to be seated at the speakers' table gathered in a room just behind the table area for awhile before the proceedings began, my wife and I had an opportunity to visit with Mr. Truman before entering the main hall. Among those present at the speakers' table, in addition to Mr. Truman, were the Vice President and Mrs. Lyndon B. Johnson; Secretary of State Dean Rusk; Supreme Court Justices Arthur R. Goldberg and Byron R. White; Senators Hubert Humphrey, Mike Mansfield, George S. McGovern, Gaylord A. Nelson, and Abraham Ribicoff; Speaker of the House Sam Rayburn, and Representative Carl Albert; Governors J. Lindsay Almond, Jr., of Virginia, Luther H. Hodges of North Carolina, and John B. Connally of Texas; and former presidential candidate Adlai E. Stevenson. At the conclusion of the dinner, Mr. Kennedy thanked me for my participation in the program, and again I was impressed with his youthful appearance and the warmth of his personality.

The only other time I had a chance to speak to the president was at the swearing-in ceremonies for former Congressman Brooks Hays at the time he became a special assistant to the president. Mr. Hays and I had been close friends for many years, and he was kind enough to include me among those he invited to the White House to witness his induction to his new duties. Among others present were Vice President Johnson; former Secretary of the Interior (in the Truman administration) Oscar L. Chapman; Dr. Paul Geren, Director of the Peace Corps and former Baptist missionary to Burma; Dr. Clarence W. Cranford, Mr. Hays's pastor; and members of Mr. Hays's family, including his wife and mother-in-law. After he had taken his oath of office, Mr. Hays was given an opportunity to speak. After expressing his appreciation for the honor of serving the president, Mr. Hays, in his best humorous style, declared: "Someone has said that behind every man who amounts to something is his wife who always knew he would succeed, and his mother-in-law who is surprised!" Then he added: "My mother-in-law is surprised that I am not president!" After Mr. Hays had concluded his remarks, the president mingled among the guests and spoke to each one present. Mr. Hays took Dr. Cranford and me over to where the president was standing, and jokingly said: "Mr. President, I want you to know that these two constitute the Baptist hierarchy of Washington!" The president was amused at this use of Catholic terminology, but "Cranny" and I knew better than to assume such eminence.

I was conducting the funeral service of a former serviceman at the time Mr. Kennedy was shot in Dallas. We had just driven into Arlington Cemetery and stopped near the gravesite when the undertaker walked over to the car and told us that he had just heard on his car radio that the president had been shot but that the seriousness of his condition had not yet been determined. The news was so startling that it was difficult to complete the service.

When we returned to the car, the radio announcer in Dallas was still uncertain as to the extent of the president's wounds but as we drove back into Washington, it became increasingly evident that the situation was grave indeed. By the time we reached the downtown business section of the city, the dreaded word was given. I went immediately to our church and assisted one of our staff members in draping black bunting around the main entrance to the building. I recall that while we were doing this, a stranger stopped to say how fine he thought it was for a Baptist Church to show such distress over the death of a Roman Catholic. The remark seemed terribly strange to me since Mr. Kennedy was the president of us all, and those of us who had been privileged to have even casual contacts with him felt that we had lost a special friend. In fact, I have never seen an entire city grieve as Washington grieved during those tragic days. I had seen the tears among the people who lined the streets when Mr. Roosevelt's body was brought back to Washington from Warm Springs, Georgia, but the grief for Mr. Kennedy was of a different nature. Mr. Roosevelt had lived a long and eventful life—his historic achievements were behind him; Mr. Kennedy was struck down in his young manhood with so much to look forward to in the future.

On the Sunday between the president's assassination on Friday and his burial on Monday, my sermon topic was, "Who Is Guilty?" and a summary of the message is as follows:

It isn't easy to answer the question, "Who is responsible for the President's death?" for few crimes are unrelated, isolated instances of personal guilt. The truly sensitive person will find it impossible to detach himself completely from the various factors which were a part of this tragic event. Holy Scripture speaks of several kinds of indirect but related guilt: the guilt of neglect by which otherwise good men become so involved in trite things that they neglect weightier matters; guilt by attempted disengagement, as when Pilate washed his hands and thereby sought to evade his rightful responsibilities; guilt by silence, as when Simon Peter warmed himself by the fire which had been kindled by the enemies of Christ, and uttered not a word in our Lord's defense; and guilt by spiritual blindness and insensitivity, as is illustrated by the reference of Jesus to those in the last judgment who will express surprise at any suggestion that they have neglected him while showing no concern for the plight of "the least of these, my brethren."

Our young and able president was slain by an assassin's bullet, but numerous hands may have helped to pull the trigger. The guilt must be shared by all who glorify violence in any form; by those who are either too selfish or too busy to recognize the importance of healthy family relationships. It would be interesting to know more about the young man who has been charged with the crime. Did he receive the love and understanding in his early years at home which are every child's right, or was he so mistreated that he grew up with a chip on his shoulder and rebellion in his heart? The guilt must also be shared by those who are quick to offer criticism of our country while accepting without question the propaganda of other nations. The accused young man in Dallas identified himself as a "Marxist" who had once sought citizenship in the Soviet Union. The guilt is shared, too, by those who make careless and irresponsible charges of treason against all who do not share their personal conclusions. In an atmosphere of reckless accusation whether from the "far left" or the "far right," emotionally and mentally disturbed persons become distraught and do irrational things. And finally, the guilt must be shared by all who encourage blind and irresponsible partisanship. In recent weeks we have had a foretaste of the quadrennial orgy of political charge and counter-charge through which our country passes in what is called "an effort to maintain the two-party system." Surely there must be some better way in which to do this.

The Christian, confronted by any tragic occurrence, can either say with the Pharisee of old, "Lord, I thank thee that I am not like other men," or he can say with the discerning Publican, "Lord, be merciful to me, a sinner."

The next day at noon, while St. Matthew's Cathedral was

packed with members of the Cabinet, Supreme Court justices, members of Congress, and foreign dignitaries attending the funeral services, our church and some others in the city, held separate memorial services. Since our church is only a few blocks from St. Matthew's, and our service was brief, our people were later able to join the throngs on the streets to observe the impressive procession on foot from the Cathedral to Arlington Cemetery. The presence of General de Gaulle and other distinguished persons walking in the procession, underscored the world-wide implications of this tragedy.

That afternoon, following the funeral services, the new president, Lyndon B. Johnson, received the foreign dignitaries in one of the large reception rooms at the State Department and undertook to reassure them that no major changes in our foreign policy were anticipated.

I had met Mr. Johnson for the first time on the floor of the Senate the same day that I had met Mr. Kennedy. Later, after he became president, I met him again at the Texas State dinner in Washington at which I had been asked to give the invocation. Mr. Johnson arrived midway through the dinner and walked down the entire distance of the speakers' table, shaking hands with each person there. When the dinner had been concluded, he spoke briefly, indicating some of the agony through which he was passing in those early days of the Vietnamese conflict. My wife and I were sitting near Bill Moyers[1] and his wife, and were able to learn from them how true to the facts the president's words were. They said that when everyone in the White House had gone to bed or gone home, the president would remain up, listening for word that the American flyers had returned to their bases safely, and would be terribly depressed if one of them was lost.

Mr. and Mrs. Johnson were members of the Christian Church (Disciples of Christ) and attended the National City Christian Church in Washington, though he would visit some

1. The president's press secretary.

other church for a special occasion. One of his White House staff, Mr. Marvin Watson, also a Texan, was a deacon in our church, and he and his wife were very conscientious in their attendance at church and participation in its activities. One Saturday morning, Mr. Watson called me at my home and said that Dr. Billy Graham and his teenage son were to be President Johnson's guests over the weekend and might be coming to our church the next morning. He promised to let me know definitely as soon as plans for the next day were completed. That afternoon, he called again to say that they were definitely coming.

The next morning we reserved an entire pew for the president and his party, and while we did not announce at the first service that there would be distinguished guests at the second service, word got around, and many of those who had been present at 9:30 returned at 11:00. Some of these met the presidential party at the entrance to the church and greeted them before they entered the sanctuary. Included in the group were President and Mrs. Johnson; their daughter, Lynda Bird; Dr. Graham and his son; and Mr. and Mrs. Watson. The sermon I had prepared for that day was entitled "The Missing Word," and that word was "conversion." It seemed to me that this was an appropriate message, at least when an evangelist was present, though the content of the sermon had been determined before learning of the visit of the president and Dr. Graham.

In the announcement period, I extended words of welcome to the president and his family, and to Dr. Graham and his son, assuring the evangelist of our prayers as he prepared to leave for Australia for a major crusade. Then, as I would on any Sunday, I announced that members of the congregation were invited to remain after the service for a coffee hour in the fellowship hall downstairs. When the sermon had been concluded, and the final hymn had been sung, I requested, as I had always done when Mr. Truman was present, that the congregation remain seated after the benediction until the president and his party had left the sanctuary. Then I pronounced the benediction and walked down to the president's pew, expecting him to get up and walk out with me. Instead, he remained seated. I leaned over to see why he had not stood, and he whispered to me: "We are staying for the coffee hour." I told him that this would be fine, but that we would go to the fellowship hall from the vestibule after leaving the sanctuary. Then he stood, as did the rest of his party, and we walked together down the center aisle to the main door. When we reached the vestibule, it was teeming with people who had heard that the president was in church. We then moved toward the stairwell which led to the hall downstairs, and it, too, was crowded with people.

I was momentarily at a loss to know what to do since I supposed that this was the sort of situation which would be disturbing to the Secret Service. I turned to one of them and sought instructions and he indicated that I should go right ahead and the president would follow. I think he must have shaken every hand that was extended to him as we descended the stairs. Within a few minutes of reaching the hall, two large circles of people were formed—one around the president and another around Dr. Graham. Both of them reacted to the situation as though it were "old-home week" and no one seemed in a hurry to leave. As I was accompanying Mr. Johnson to the sidewalk later, he picked up the small son of the Watsons, and it was with the little boy in his arms that we reached the exit to the street and were greeted by news photographers. The following week, I received a letter from the president, saying: "It was a privilege for my family and me to worship with you. Our sense of comfort and encouragement is deepened by the knowledge that we have your understanding and are remembered in your prayers."

During the coffee hour I had introduced our son to the president, and mentioned that he was a page in the Senate, having been appointed by Senator Yarborough of Texas. The next Sunday, when Senator Yarborough spoke to me after the morning service, he said: "Last Sunday, when the president got back to the White House after attending services here, he called me on the telephone and said: 'Yarborough, what are you doing with a page who isn't from Texas?'" The senator then declared that he had offered what he thought was a reasonable explanation but that he got the definite impression that the president wanted him to get a Texan as his page. As a consequence, our son was shifted to a more responsible position so that a Texas boy might be invited to Washington.

This little incident reminded me of the story that went the rounds in Washington after Mr. Johnson had made his first TV address after becoming president. It seems that an elderly Texas lady listened to him intently and then commented: "Thank goodness we have at last a president who doesn't have an accent!" On the contrary, you couldn't be around Mr. Johnson very long without realizing that he had a distinct Texas accent, in more ways than one!

In the last year of his administration, Mr. Johnson appointed Mr. Watson to be the Postmaster General of the United States. We were invited to the Rose Garden of the White House for the swearing-in ceremonies and to a memorable buffet luncheon served in the garden under a cloudless sky. I was further impressed with the thoughtfulness of President and Mrs. Johnson when they sent me a basket of flowers from the White House while I was in the hospital recuperating from a heart attack.

Mr. Nixon was inaugurated just a few weeks before I retired. My only contacts with him were on those occasions when I opened the Senate with prayer and, as vice president, he would present me for the invocation.

X

VENTURES IN INTERPRETATION

Numerous experiences in the past, as well as current situations I was facing, helped to crystallize the impression that possibly my major contribution to the religious climate of our time could be made in the role of an interpreter. When I was nearing the end of my seminary years in Louisville, I discussed with our president, Dr. E. Y. Mullins, the possibility of going abroad for graduate study. He suggested that I go to Edinburgh and study under Dr. Hugh Ross Mackintosh, saying that he considered Dr. Mackintosh to be the foremost theologian in the English-speaking world at the time. He then went on to say that he had become acquainted with the Scottish theologian during World War I when Dr. Mackintosh was assigned the responsibility of interpreting America and the American servicemen to British troops, and Dr. Mullins had been assigned to a similar task in interpreting Great Britain and the British troops to American soldiers. If the young men of the two countries were to form any effective united front against a common enemy, they would have to give up their presuppositions and prejudices regarding one another. I never forgot that conversation. What had been said about understanding and cooperation in wartime seemed to me to have significant implications for the world of religion, and I desired to have some part in helping men to find the essential elements of their unity as the children of God.

This desire received an added sense of urgency when I became pastor of a church in Washington that maintained relationships with both of our national conventions. Having been reared and largely educated in the South, I was thoroughly acquainted with the work of Southern Baptists. While pursuing graduate work at Yale and Edinburgh, I became better acquainted with the work of Northern and British Baptists. The University of Shanghai in which I taught for a year was supported jointly by Northern and Southern Baptists, and therefore the teaching staff was made up of personnel from both Conventions. All of these experiences had prepared me to work with both Conventions and to serve as an interpreter between the two. Whenever I was invited to speak in a northern church, and while serving on the Foreign Mission Board of the Northern Convention, I would seek an opportunity to interpret Southern Baptists to those present; and when speaking in southern churches, and while serving on the Executive Committee of the Southern Convention, I sought opportunities to interpret Northern Baptists to those present. When I was elected president of the Northern Convention in Boston in 1950, new opportunities were provided me for pursuing this ministry of interpretation. The more I came to know Baptists in the North, the more I became convinced that the great body of Baptists, North and South, are remarkably similar in spirit, in dedication, and even in theological convictions.

In recent years, the leaders of both Conventions have become better acquainted with one another through mutual participation in the annual meetings of the Executive Committee of the Baptist World Alliance and its study commissions, and through participation in the activities of the North American Baptist Fellowship. In the process of taking part in these joint ventures, many of the key personalities in both Conventions have come to see how unfounded were some of the misgivings and apprehensions they had previously entertained regarding one another. These meetings have truly been reconciling and healing experiences.

My greater understanding of other evangelical

denominations came through joint efforts in Washington to meet the spiritual needs of the thousands in Washington who had left hometowns all over America and were now employed in government agencies. Occasionally, too, I had the opportunity to attend international and interdenominational conferences in this country and abroad, and in the year that I served as president of the American Baptist Convention,[1] I had the privilege of signing the charter of the National Council of Churches for my denomination.

At a World Council of Churches meeting in Sweden, distinguished prelates were housed in dormitory rooms at the University of Uppsala along with laymen and pastors, and we all rode the bus together from the dormitories to the assembly hall. In this way, the delegates had an opportunity to become better acquainted with one another and to acquire the sense of oneness that is so essential to any religious gathering. The wives of the delegates also got to know one another as they sat together in the visitors' section of the assembly hall or as they were escorted on tours which had been arranged by the church women of Sweden. On the opening day of the Council's sessions, a service of worship was held in the beautiful Uppsala Cathedral. King Gustaf and members of the royal family were present, and a special musical composition had been commissioned for the service. As the delegates entered the Cathedral, the music which was being offered in worship was almost beyond description. The commissioned composition was being presented by two large choirs, accompanied by two pipe organs, trumpeters, and other instrumental musicians, and the pealing of the great Cathedral bells in the towers. As I write these words, my spine tingles at the memory of it all. And in addition to the beauty of the church and the magnificence of the music, there was the awareness that here were gathered men and women from many tongues and nations, high church and low church, Eastern Orthodox arch-

---

1. The year I was elected president, the name of the convention was changed from Northern to American.

bishops in tall black hats, with jeweled crosses hanging from chains around their necks, and Quakers and Pentacostals in their simple dress, but all recognizing Jesus Christ as Lord and Savior and coming together to worship the God and Father of us all. Again and again I was reminded of the words of Scripture: "And they shall come from the north and the south, the east and the west, and sit down in the kingdom of God."

Before the delegates entered the Cathedral, their wives were permitted to enter and occupy a section of seats reserved for them. After my wife had been seated, an attractive, youth-ful-looking lady entered and sat down next to her. Politely, she leaned over to my wife and whispered, "I am . . . Ramsey." Being a musician, and momentarily caught up in the overwhelming beauty of the music, my wife came back to earth and whispered back, "So nice to meet you. I am Mae Pruden from America." Not until later, after the music had ceased, did she connect the British accent with Ramsey and realize that she was sitting next to the wife of the archbiship of Canterbury. Other contacts with her confirmed what a personable and gracious lady she really was. The archbishop, riding the bus in his purple robe and chatting animatedly with all and sundry, was a sight we shall not soon forget.

My venture in interpretation with Roman Catholics began in meetings of this kind where they were observers, but took a rather dramatic turn when I found a Jesuit priest waiting for me when I entered my study one morning several years later. The priest was Father David Bowman, a member of the faculty at Catholic University in Washington. He said that he had seen the newspaper account of my refusal to be identified with those who were opposed to Senator Kennedy's nomination for the presidency on the basis of his religion, and that he had concluded that I would be the kind of person who would be receptive to the promotion of greater understanding between Catholics and Protestants. I assured him that nothing would please me more, and we enjoyed an extended visit together. I was deeply impressed with him and felt that this was a person I would like very much to know better. As he stood to leave, he asked whether or not I would be willing to come over to Catholic University and explain the Baptist position to his students. I was, of course, delighted to accept his invitation, and shall never forget the warm and responsive reception I received from his students—young nuns, priests, and lay students. They listened attentively, asked relevant questions, and altogether it was, for me at least, a very satisfying experience. To my delight, Father Bowman had me return for other visits, and we became close friends.

The next year when the anniversary of our church was approaching, I invited Father Bowman to be the principal speaker at our annual dinner. I have an idea that he thought this was going to be just another church supper because as he entered the banquet hall and found occupants of the head table in evening clothes, and over four hundred people present, he seemed a bit surprised. However, he was soon very much a part of the occasion. When he stood to speak, it was interesting to see the eager faces of those present who had never heard a Catholic priest speak in a Baptist Church. They seemed to be leaning forward in their efforts to be hospitable and receptive. Father Bowman seemed equally anxious to establish a meeting ground on which those of differing traditions might mingle as brothers and sisters in Christ, and he succeeded to a remarkable degree. At the end of the dinner, a long line formed to express appreciation and to voice the hope that he would visit us again.

The next year, while planning our list of speakers for our Lenten services held on Wednesday nights in the sanctuary, I decided to invite Father Bowman to be one of these. He readily accepted. About two weeks before he was to appear, I got a telephone call from a lady who identified herself as a staff member in the diocesan office of the Catholic church in Washington. She said that she had heard that Father Bowman was scheduled to speak in our church soon, and she wanted to know if I had received the bishop's permission, declaring emphatically that such permission *was* necessary, and that it looked as though we had a problem. Then she inquired as to the nature of the service. Thinking back quickly over some past experiences I had had with services in which both Catholics and Protestants were involved, I recalled that a "prayer vigil" was considered by the Catholics to be an informal gathering and not a formal service of worship. I knew that any service in a Baptist church would appear informal to Catholics, so I said: "Oh, I would say that the service to which Father Bowman has been invited is something like a 'prayer vigil.' " The lady seemed somewhat relieved and said that if I would write a letter to the bishop explaining this fact she felt sure she could get it approved. I wrote the letter and the invitation was approved. I then wrote to Father Bowman who was then the only Roman Catholic on the staff of the National Council of Churches in New York, and said: "Dear Dave: You *were* going to speak at a Lenten service in our church, but now you are going to speak at a prayer vigil. However, I don't think the Lord will notice the difference!" His message on the night he spoke was an impressive delineation of the theological assumptions upon which he believed both Baptists and Catholics confront the world—the authority of Scripture, the Lordship of Christ, and religious freedom.

Early in my Washington experience, I had become acquainted with Rabbi Norman Gerstenfeld, spiritual leader of the Washington Hebrew Congregation. In the course of time, we became good friends through our contacts on various interfaith civic committees. I once called him on the telephone to inquire as to where I might find some unleavened bread to use in our Maunday Thursday communion service. He replied that he would like very much to provide this for me and would see that it was delivered the next day. The next day his wife drove up to the front of the church and brought in enough unleavened bread to last us for several months. Before that supply was exhausted, she came again with additional boxes of bread. Each year the rabbi would send his confirmation class, a group of seventy-five or so teenagers, to a morning service of our church. We would be informed in advance as to the Sunday they would like to come, and reserve seats for them, and plan to include in the service features which would permit the young people to participate. For instance, we would sing, "The God of Abraham praise," or "O God our help in ages past"; the responsive reading would be from the Psalms; and usually I would speak on a theme which would underscore our common spiritual heritage or stress some of the things we ought to be doing togther as persons possessing a vital faith in the living God. At the close of the service, the young people would remain in their seats and I would go to them to answer any questions they might have regarding the service or the Baptist theological position. After attempting to provide answers to their questions, I would point to the Old Testament characters depicted in our Great Window over the main entrance to the church—Abraham, Moses, and Isaiah— and point out that we considered these men of God to be among *our* spiritual ancestors too.

Rabbi Gerstenfeld was a member of the Reformed branch of his faith and a man of broad sympathies. On one occasion he had as his house guest the minister of Cults of the State of Israel where only Orthodox Judaism is practiced. He invited some of us to tea at his home so that we might have the opportunity of meeting his guest from Israel. As we went down the receiving line, I finally reached the visiting Israeli cabinet member, and when the rabbi introduced me to him and explained that I was a Baptist minister, the Israeli visitor said: "We have only a few Baptists in Israel, but they are giving us some trouble." When I inquired as to the nature of the trouble, he replied: "They are translating the works of Roger Williams on religious liberty into the language of our people and thereby creating quite a bit of unrest." The rabbi was standing by listening to the conversation, and he exclaimed: "Good for them!" I was then reminded that the rabbi had named his oldest son Roger William Gerstenfeld. Certainly there could be no more eloquent expression of appreciation of the struggle of Roger Williams for the rights of minorities than the rabbi's decision to name his son for this apostle of religious freedom.

Washington also provided unsurpassed opportunities for an interpreter in the area of race relations. Not only was the percentage of black residents in the city growing rapidly, but the civil rights movement began to receive the attention it should have received long ago. While I thoroughly recognized the necessity of the enactment of certain legal guarantees to equal citizenship for all, I felt that as a Christian minister my best contribution to the movement could be made stressing the spiritual dimensions resident in the concepts of human dignity, the sacredness of human personality, and the God-given rights of all men to find fulfillment. I encouraged the creation of a monthly joint meeting of the black and white ministers of our denomination; the reception of the first black church into our D.C. Baptist Convention; the exchange of pulpits and choirs with a neighboring black church; and invitations to black speakers to share our midweek dinner and speak at the service that followed. Our church joined other downtown churches in publishing in the daily press a list of the churches that were open to all races.

After the Supreme Court decision of 1954 which struck down segregated schools, I knew that we could no longer take for granted that we were ready to receive black Christians who might apply for membership, but that we should deal with the matter specifically as a matter of principle before a personality should become involved. Certainly there was nothing in our constitution to suggest exclusion on account of race, but this was not enough. One night I called together our diaconate—approximately fifty men and women—and explained that while I knew what I wanted to do if a black Christian requested membership in our church, I also wanted to be sure that I had their backing in doing what I regarded as the only Christian thing to do. I then suggested that it was rather late in the day for anyone in our church to consider setting up racial barriers since we had had every race of mankind in the congregation during the one hundred and fifty years of the church's history. During the first forty years there had been numerous slaves within the memberhsip. Since that time we have received Chinese, Burmese, Indians, and people from the world over.

Then I said that it would be egotistical for us to assume that a completely open-door policy would result in a great surge of black applicants who were eager to worship with us. I pointed out that our black Baptists had some great churches in Washington; they had ways of worship which were just as precious to them as ours were to us; and if we put a sign on the front lawn begging them to come, only a few would respond. Then I concluded: ''Whose church is this, anyway? Does it belong to us or to Christ? Do we provide the guidelines for membership in a New Testament church, or are they in the Word of God? Are the conditions for church membership sociological or theological?'' Within a moment or two I sat down and waited to see what response I would get.

I shall always be thankful that the first deacon to get to his feet was from Mississippi—Sam Jones. He said he thought that what the pastor had said was right, and that if a black man came forward in our church and requested membership, he wanted to have the privilege of being the first to go to him and shake his hand, assuring him of a warm welcome. The next to get to his feet was John Shouse from Kentucky, and in similar words he voiced his complete endorsement of Mr. Jones's sentiments. The next was Paul Creasman from Tennessee and he, too, expressed the hope that the group would support the pastor in his refusal to countenance racism anywhere in the life of the church. In a moment, someone moved that this be the sense of the body, and a rising vote was taken. Almost everyone stood. I later related this incident to the congregation at a Sunday morning service; and when our first black applicant for membership came forward a few months later, it was taken as a matter of course, and he was given a warm welcome. While the number of black members has never been large, we now have two serving as deacons and others have rendered valuable service in the choir. While the March on Washington and Martin Luther King's stirring address seemed to be the turning point in civil rights progress elsewhere in the nation, many of the proposed changes in race relations had already taken place in the capital city. This, of

135

course, was given tremendous impetus by the fair employment practices of the government agencies in Washington.

In bringing this chapter to a conclusion, I shall simply mention in passing the opportunity of helping to interpret the ideals of the free world to the Iron Curtain countries while serving as the Protestant representative on the Religious Advisory Committee of the Voice of America; the privilege of trying to relate the implications of the Christian faith to congressional decisions as I spoke Sunday after Sunday to members of Congress and other public officials who attended our services; the inspiration of sharing with young people in more than thirty colleges, universities, and seminaries my own convictions regarding the relevance of the message of Christ to the issues of our time; and the satisfaction of witnessing the response of American servicemen as I participated in several preaching missions to the personnel of the Armed Services in Alaska, Europe, and here at home. I knew through it all, however, that the best interpretation of the Christian faith is not to be found in words but in the quality of a person's life, and so my major concern was to exemplify in a pastoral ministry the ideal I recommended from the pulpit. While I did not always succeed in this, I believe my hearers knew that this was the goal I was striving to reach.

Looking back now on those thirty-two years in our nation's capital, I am aware that I received far more than I gave, and shall always be grateful for the enriching experiences which came to me, and to my family, through contacts with many wonderful and interesting people; through witnessing and participating in numerous historic occasions; and through the broadening influences which such a cosmopolitan atmosphere provides. Our country has passed through many critical periods, and it will encounter others in the years ahead, but in Washington there is, and always will be, the "saving salt" which is so essential to the survival of a nation.

THE END